BIRDS' NESTS

A Field Guide

Birges

RICHARD HEADSTROM

BIRDS' NESTS

A Field Guide

An identification manual to
the nests of birds of the United States
east of the one hundredth meridian

IVES WASHBURN, INC.   NEW YORK

To My Wife

with Gratitude

Printed in the United States of America

Foreword to the Third Printing

AT THE offices of the National Audubon Society, we have a persistently challenging problem of trying to help people identify the nests of birds. Men, women, and children occasionally send us the old or abandoned nests of birds; more often, they write us letters from many parts of the country or telephone from close by to describe a nest to us. What bird built it, they want to know, and how can they learn to identify birds' nests for themselves? We tell them there is no *easy way*, no more than in learning to identify birds. Skill in nest identification, as in identifying birds, comes with practice.

One of the first things we ask our questioners is to describe *where* they saw the nest. Was it on the ground in an open field or in the woods; in a tree or in a bush; and if in a tree or a bush, how high from the ground, etc. After the general questioning, we try to narrow our search (for search it is) to the approximate size of the nest, its depth, its outside and inside diameter, the materials with which it was built, and so on.

However, until we had for reference Richard Headstrom's *Birds' Nests, a Field Guide,* I am afraid that much of our questioning was haphazard.

During our discussion of birds' nests, we always ask our correspondents that the nest they have found be left undisturbed. We do not encourage nest collecting. People may unknowingly collect a nest that is partly built, or recently completed, just before the eggs are laid. Sometimes birds will use the same nest after the first brood has flown. Collections of nests also take up a lot of space. They are interesting and useful for reference in natural history museums, but unless they are taken by skilled collectors after the bird nesting season is over and kept in special drawers or under glass, they are usually dust collectors in private homes and are eventually thrown out. I think that anyone who has access to Mr. Headstrom's book will not need to collect a nest to identify the builder, or to make a collection of nests for reference. *Birds' Nests, a Field Guide* is the most helpful book on the subject I know of, and I recommend it to all those people whose curiosity about a bird's nest will always make them stop and say, "I wonder who built it?"

JOHN K. TERRES
Editor Audubon Magazine

Preface

WHEN Richard Headstrom wrote a series of articles covering the identification of birds' nests for The Bulletin of the Massachusetts Audubon Society a few years ago, we had no idea how useful this key would prove to be. The articles were reprinted and were immediately in demand by teachers and youth leaders throughout the State, and we even had calls for them from other States. Consequently, when Mr. Headstrom asked our advice about having this material published in book form, extending it to cover all species in the United States east of the Rocky Mountains, we gave enthusiastic endorsement to the idea.

When snow covers the ground and trees are bare, students of nature lore delight to investigate exposed birds' nests and try to discover the identity of the builders. Mr. Headstrom's volume should now remove much of the guesswork in identifying nests and lead to increased enjoyment of bird-watchers everywhere as they add this interesting sideline to their hobby. We believe, too, that camp counselors, teachers, and others will find this material of real value in their work with children.

C. Russell Mason
Executive Director
Massachusetts Audubon Society

Acknowledgements

I WANT to express my grateful appreciation to Mr. C. Russell Mason of the Massachusetts Audubon Society whose co-operation and encouragement helped to make this volume possible; to the following for permission to use their photographs: Martin K. Bovey, Roland Campbell, Robert L. Coffin, Allan D. Cruickshank, Grice and Grice, S. A. Grimes, Alfred O. Gross, Hal H. Harrison, Ralph E. Lawrence, Wm. H. Lawrence, Roger T. Peterson, Ruth Turner, and Lawrence H. Walkinshaw; and to my wife who ably assisted in the preparation of the manuscript.

Contents

Nests On or In the Ground

I. In Fields or Pastures

II. In Woods

9

III. In Marshes

IV. On or Near Seashore and Lake Beaches

V. In Burrows in the Ground

VII. Containing Twigs or Sticks

VIII. In Holes in Trees or Stumps, in Birdhouses or Similar Places

IX. In or On Buildings

Index of Birds

15

Introduction

TO THOSE who are interested in birds or wildlife in general the title of this book should convey a subtle challenge, for how many of us know as much as we should about birds' nests? How many of us can identify a nest with a reasonable degree of accuracy after it has served its purpose and the birds have departed?

I think the subject is a fascinating one. I also think it is a phase of bird study which has been very much neglected. If you do not agree with me, let me suggest that you go to the nearest field, orchard, or woods and see if you can name the maker of the first empty nest you find. In this way you may discover a new sphere of interest, even a new hobby.

Birds build nests in which to incubate their eggs and to serve as a cradle for their young until they are able to care for themselves. Accordingly, it is not surprising to find that birds select sites for their nests with the greatest care and build them, as a rule, in inaccessible places or where they will be most completely hidden. Some go to great lengths to conceal their nests. The Meadowlark and some sparrows arch their nests over with growing vegetation. The Ovenbird covers its nest with dry leaves from the forest floor where it rests. The Ruby-throated Hummingbird and the Wood Pewee, which are unusually adept in the art of camouflage, cover their nests with lichens so that they appear to be excrescences on the branch of the tree.

Nests are placed in almost every conceivable location. The Song Sparrow may build its nest beneath a tuft of grass, the Great Blue Heron in the tallest tree, the Chimney Swift in a chimney, the Yellow Warbler in a low bush, the Black-capped Chickadee in a decaying stump, the House Sparrow in an electric-light hood or waterspout, the Osprey on the crossbar of a telegraph pole, the Crested Flycatcher in a hole in a tree, the Kingfisher in a burrow in a sandbank, and the House Wren in the most unlikely places—even in an old tin can, the fold of a blanket hanging on a clothesline, or the burrow in a bank made by a Bank Swallow for its nesting.

Some birds build very crude nests. The Mourning Dove, for instance, builds merely a loose platform of twigs. The Yellow-billed Cuckoo does slightly better, but its nest is still little more than a shallow, frail platform, so loosely constructed that the eggs appear to be in danger of falling out through the interstices. On the other hand, the Robin builds a bulky, compact, thick-walled nest of mud, reinforced with grass and straw. In contrast to these, there are the dainty, trim nest of the Ruby-throated Hummingbird and the exquisitely woven structure of the Baltimore Oriole, perhaps the finest examples of native bird architecture.

Some birds make only a slight pretense at building a nest. The Killdeer deposits its eggs in a crudely lined hollow in the ground, and this method is also followed by the Spotted Sandpiper and the Upland Plover. The Whip-poor-will lays its eggs among dead leaves, as if it were aware that its eggs resemble so closely the color and pattern of the forest floor that only with difficulty can they be discovered. The woodpeckers place their eggs in natural holes in trees or in holes they excavate. They have discovered, perhaps, that in such hiding places their eggs are comparatively safe—except against such enemies as squirrels and snakes. Some birds, like the Cowbird, lay their eggs in the nest of a bird of another species and leave the raising of the young to the foster parents.

All kinds of materials are used in nest-building. Many birds, like the Grasshopper and Field Sparrows, use grass. The hawks and herons build their nests of sticks and twigs. The Red-eyed Vireo uses strips of bark, bits of dead wood, paper, and the down of plants. The Robin and the Phoebe use mud, and the Parula Warbler weaves a nest of usnea already hanging from the tree limb. The Goldfinch lines its nest characteristically with thistle-down, the Barn Swallow with poultry feathers.

Materials are likely to be chosen according to their availability. A Chipping Sparrow, for example, lined her nest with fine wire rather than the customary horsehair, and Crested Flycatchers now frequently pick up cellophane cigar wrappers as a substitute for the cast snake-skin.

Birds not only make use of a wide variety of materials and often display great ingenuity in nest-building, but they also readily adapt themselves to varying or changing environmental conditions. The Red-wing will build a much deeper nest in a place subjected to strong winds than in a sheltered location. The Chimney Swift now builds in our chimneys in preference to the hollow trees in which it formerly nested, and we find the Phoebe and the Barn Swallow making use of man-made structures, whereas they originally built their nests on rocks.

Most birds nest singly, but a few, like the Purple Martin and some of the swallows, herons, terns, and gulls, nest in colonies. To these colony nesters might be added the Bobolink, the Red-wing, and the Marsh Wren, which nest in somewhat scattered communities. As a rule, birds build nests for just one season. Most individuals that survive the winter return the following season to the same nesting site, but only a few species may use the same nest year after year. Certain owls are known to use the same hole for years in succession, and crows and hawks often rebuild their old nests.

In attempting to identify a birds' nest, with the owners absent, it must be remembered that, although birds of a given species follow a fairly consistent pattern in nest construction, individual builders frequently depart from the general species rule both as to location selected and materials used. A Blue Jay was found building on a tree root projecting from an overhanging eroded bank, instead of in the usual pine tree. A Hermit Thrush used a hole in a haystack for its nest instead of the crevice of a rocky, wooded bank. Flickers have been known to drill their nesting holes through the outer wall of ice-houses and deposit the eggs on the sawdust insulation between the outer and inner wall. Birds that commonly nest on the ground may choose a low shrub or brier bush, or vice versa.

On the whole, nests can best be identified by finding the birds at home, yet there are certain general characteristics as to material used, location, and size which make most nests possible of identification, even when found at other times than the breeding season. The Chipping Sparrow, as already mentioned, usually lines its nest with horsehair, the Barn Swallow with feathers, and the Goldfinch with thistledown, while the Catbird may be expected to use grapevine bark in the main part of the nest, and the Ruby-throated Hummingbird and the Wood Pewee will cover the exterior with lichens. This guide is an attempt to help those who enjoy nest-hunting to identify nests with some measure of success, especially during the winter months in the North, when many nests are easy to see. And since bird life and plant life are then at their lowest ebb for observation, another objective will add interest to our winter trips.

How to Use This Book

THE FIRST thing to consider in identifying a nest is the kind of environment in which it is built—marsh, swamp, field, woods, or orchard. After that observe its location—whether it is placed on or in the ground or in a bush or tree. If the nest is on the ground, note the exact site, that is, is it in or beneath a tussock of grass, among the branches of a bush or beneath it, in shrubbery or beneath a boulder. If the nest is in a tree or bush, note the part of the tree or bush where it is placed and how far it is above the ground. Next, give attention to the type of nest. Is it open or closed? Is it shaped like a cup, saucer, gourd, or platform? A note should also be made as to its exact position. It may be suspended from a branch or saddled on it, or it may be placed in a crotch. The size and depth are also factors that will help in identification. Finally, observe the materials of which the nest is made.

To illustrate the use of the Key let us take two hypothetical nests and determine their identity. Our first nest is one that we chance upon while walking through a field. We find it on the ground and hence we turn to Nests On or In the Ground. Examining this division of the Key we find that it is subdivided into six sections: I. In Fields or Pastures; II. In Woods; III. In Marshes; IV. On or Near Seashore and Lake Beaches; V. In Burrows in the Ground; and VI. On Rocks or Rocky Ledges. Since our hypothetical nest is in a field we turn to Section I. In Fields or Pastures. Studying our Key we learn that section I is divided into two divisions, namely: A. Open Nest; and B. Arched Nest. We examine our hypothetical nest and note that it is of open construction. Studying our Key further we discover that we have a number of choices, all dealing with location, such as: a(1). In or under a tussock of grass; a(2). In tall grasses; a(3). Under a thistle, small bush, or weed stalk; a(4). Under low, thick bushes or growth of sprouts and briers; a(5). In a depression of the ground; and a(6). On flat ground, in slight depression, or on a flat roof of building. We carefully note the location of our hypothetical nest and observe that it had been built in a brier growth. Turning to a(4) we find that we have three possibilities; in other words, that our hypothetical nest was made by the Palm Warbler, the Clay-colored Sparrow, or the Field Sparrow. We study the descriptions carefully and again examine our hypothetical nest, whereupon we find that our nest contains weed stems and rootlets. As only the description of the nest of the Field Sparrow mentions weed stems and rootlets we conclude that the maker of our hypothetical nest was the Field Sparrow.

Our second hypothetical nest is one we find in a small sapling while strolling through the woods. As this nest is above the ground we turn to Nests Above the Ground, which we find is subdivided into nine sections; I. Hanging or Semihanging; II. Covered on Outside with Lichens and Saddled on Branch; III. Felted Nests of Cottony Materials; IV. Containing a Layer of Mud; V. Made Chiefly of Bark, Fibers, Twigs, and Rootlets; VI. Made Chiefly of Grasses, Rootlets, Leaves, and Straw; VII. Containing Twigs or Sticks; VIII. In Holes in Trees or Stumps, In Birdhouses or Similar Places; and IX. In or On Buildings. Our first step, before we can proceed, is to note the location of our hypothetical nest, and since it is neither a hanging or semihanging one nor built in a hole we continue on to examine the material of which it is made. We observe that it is not covered on the outside with lichens nor is it made of cottony materials. We also find that it does not contain a layer of mud nor is it made chiefly of twigs or sticks. Thus by a process of elimination we have narrowed our possibilities down to sections V and VI. Our choice now lies between nests Made Chiefly of Bark, Fibers, Twigs, and Rootlets, and nests Made Chiefly of Grasses, Rootlets, Leaves, and Straw. At this point we again examine the materials of which our hypothetical nest is made and note that it is made chiefly of bark strips and rootlets with some fibers and a few twigs. Our choice, then, is section V. Since section V is divided into two main divisions: A. Less than 2 inches, inside diameter, and B. More than 2 inches, inside diameter, our next step is to measure * the inside diameter of our nest, which we find to be less than two inches. We must now decide between: a(1). Usually in conifers, and a (2). In bushes or saplings. As our nest has not been built in a conifer we accordingly come to a (2) where we find that we have three possibilities. Our hypothetical nest was made by the Black-throated Blue Warbler, the Chestnut-sided Warbler, or the Prairie Warbler. We study the descriptions carefully and compare them with the nest. In description 1 we note that the nest of the Black-throated Blue Warbler is "decorated exteriorly with corky bits of wood" and that there are "bits of dead wood in bottom" and since our hypothetical nest contains such bits of wood we conclude that its maker was the Black-throated Blue Warbler.

Note: The breeding ranges as given are not necessarily complete but are limited to the region covered by the Key, that is, eastern and central United States east of the one hundredth meridian.

* As the key is based, in parts, upon measurements, a tape measure is essential and should be taken on all field trips as well as a pencil and notebook for notes.

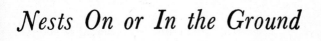

Nests On or In the Ground

I. In Fields or Pastures

A. Open Nest

a(1). In or under a tussock of grass

    1. SEE III A a(2) 2   **Mallard**

    2. Of grass, leaves, bark strips, pine needles, and moss; lined with fine rootlets or pine needles and grass; usually where pastures are overgrown with scrub; well concealed, sometimes sunk and sometimes placed in a tussock of sphagnum. [See also II A a(2) 3]

        Eastern and central United States south to Connecticut, northern New Jersey, West Virginia, northern Illinois, and Nebraska.

                Nashville Warbler

    3. Constructed principally of dried grass, with some leaves, weed stems, rootlets, and shreds of corn husks; lined with fine grass or horsehair. Usually placed on ground sheltered by a tuft of grass but sometimes placed in a small bush or tree. [See also Nests Above the Ground VI A a(1) 3 and VI B b(1) 6]

        Northwestern Minnesota, southern Michigan, and western Ohio south to southern Texas, southern Mississippi, central Alabama, and northern Georgia.

                Dickcissel

4. Of grass and fine weed stems; lined with fine grasses and vegetable down.

Western Minnesota and eastern Nebraska.
Lark Bunting

5. Bulky, of dried grass; lined with fine grass, hair, or rootlets; sometimes placed in or under a cluster of wild or cultivated plants, as strawberries or potatoes. [See also I B b(3) 2]

Southern New Hampshire, Minnesota, North Dakota south to northern Georgia, southern Louisiana, and Texas; also prairies of central Florida.
Grasshopper Sparrow

6. Of grass; lined with finer materials, hair often being used; well hidden.

Southern New Hampshire, New York, South Dakota south to North Carolina, West Virginia, and northern Texas.
Henslow's Sparrow

7. Of grasses, weeds, bark, and leaves; lined with finer materials, sometimes with rootlets or hair; sometimes built in bushes and trees and, rarely, in hollow logs, hollow trees, and nesting boxes. [See also II A a(2) 8 and Nests Above the Ground VI A a(2) 7 and VI B b(1) 9]

Eastern and central United States south to coastal North Carolina, southern Virginia, northern Georgia, southern Illinois, and Missouri.
Song Sparrow

a(2). In tall grasses
1. SEE Nests Above the Ground VII C c(4) 5
(Eastern) Ground Dove

2. Cleverly concealed. Of grasses, weed stems, and rootlets arranged in a circular form and lined with similar but finer materials; sometimes placed at the foot of a tuft of grass or bush.

Eastern and central United States south to New Jersey, West Virginia, Illinois, and northern Missouri.

Bobolink

3. A flimsy arrangement of grass and sometimes moss; lined with finer grass, hair, or rootlets.

Eastern and central United States south to northern Iowa, northern Indiana, Pennsylvania, Long Island, and the New Jersey coast.

Savannah Sparrow

4. A shallow cup-shaped cavity scratched in the dry earth among the short prairie grass in exposed places. The upper edge is sometimes rather thick and turned inward while the bottom is loosely and thinly laid; flimsy. Lined chiefly at the rim with bits of bleached grass and fine weed stalks.

North Dakota south to central Kansas, eastern Nebraska; also western Minnesota.

Chestnut-collared Longspur

a(3). Under a thistle, small bush, or weed stalk

1. Rather bulky, thick rimmed, well cupped but not tightly woven; of dried grass and rootlets lined with fine grass, rootlets, and hair.

Eastern and central United States south to North Carolina and Kentucky, Missouri and Nebraska.

Vesper Sparrow

a(4). Under low, thick bushes or growth of sprouts and briers

    1. Of grass and well lined with hair or feathers; 3 inches, external diameter; internal diameter at the top, 2 inches; outside depth, $2\frac{1}{2}$ inches; inside depth, 1 inch; placed in moss or grass at the foot of a bush or tree; sometimes in a bog in sphagnum moss at the base of a small spruce. [See also III A a(2) 11]

        Maine and northern Minnesota.

                              Palm Warbler

    2. Of grasses; lined with hair; may also be placed in bushes. [See also Nests Above the Ground VI A a(1) 5]

        Northern Nebraska, northwestern Illinois, and north-central Michigan north to Canadian border.

                          Clay-colored Sparrow

    3. Of coarse grasses, weed strips, and rootlets; lined with finer grasses and hair; often placed in a low bush, such as huckleberry or briers, only a few feet above the ground. [See also II A a(1) 15 and Nests Above the Ground VI A a(1) 6]

        Eastern and central United States south to northern parts of Gulf States.

                    (Eastern) Field Sparrow

a(5). In a depression of the ground

    1. See III A a(3) 2   **Gadwall**

    2. A slight hollow in the ground; lined with rushes, straw, grass, or stubble, and dark down.

Usually in grass or beneath a bush, invariably on dry ground, sometimes as much as a mile from water though often near water.

Canadian border south to Nebraska and Iowa and casually east to western Pennsylvania.

Pintail

3. SEE III A a(3) 6 and III A a(4) 2   **Shoveller**

4. A slight depression; thinly lined with grass and a few feathers. In open prairie country and sheltered by grass tufts or bushes.

Canadian border south to Illinois, Missouri, and Arkansas and east to Michigan and Indiana.

Prairie Chicken

5. A hollow in the ground; lined with grasses and dead leaves.

Locally in various eastern states and in Upper Mississippi Valley.

European Partridge

6. A slight natural hollow in grass or grainfield; lined scantily with leaves, grass, and straw.

Mainly north of Mason and Dixon Line (Delaware, northern Maryland, southern Ohio, southern Indiana, Missouri, and northern Oklahoma) and north to southern Maine, northern New York, southern Michigan, and Minnesota.

Ring-necked Pheasant

7. A hollow in the ground; sometimes lined with chips of stone or wood, a few pebbles or some weed stalks; or these may be scattered over

small area surrounding nesting hollow; hollow may be on bare rock with no lining.

Florida and Gulf of Mexico north to eastern and central United States.

Killdeer

8. Usually a mere depression, 4 to 5 inches in diameter and 2 to 3 inches deep, scratched in the concealment of grass from 7 to 10 inches high; lined with dried grass.

Southern Maine, Michigan, and Wisconsin south to northern Virginia and southern Illinois, southern Missouri and Oklahoma.

Upland Plover

9. Normally built in upland location, but in proximity to water. A saucer-shaped depression; usually slightly lined with dry grasses but sometimes with weed stalks or mosses; occasionally in a cavity under a large rock.

Eastern and central United States south to northern South Carolina, Alabama, and southern Louisiana.

Spotted Sandpiper

10. In short grass fields; of grass; often lined with thistledown and a few feathers; woven solidly to withstand the strong winds of early spring.

Eastern and central United States south to North Carolina, West Virginia, Missouri, and Kansas; also coast of Texas.

Horned Lark

11. Cup-shaped, generally sunk in a hollow and carefully concealed by tufts of grass or clover;

built mostly of grasses and lined with rootlets, fine grass, and long hairs. Sometimes repairs and uses abandoned nests of other birds. Occasionally built in a low tree or bush. [See also Nests Above the Ground VI A a(2) 6 and VI B b(1) 7]

Fields and pastures and open knolls of Mississippi Valley south to Texas and Louisiana, and east to Ohio and northwestern West Virginia; also a colony in Michigan.

(Eastern) Lark Sparrow

a(6). On flat ground, in slight depression

  1. No nesting material added. On gravel beaches, rocky knolls, or open barren fields unobstructed by tall shrubbery or trees, often on burned-over areas; also on flat, gravel roofs in towns and cities. May be no depression, or slight depression may be incidentally made by shoving aside of material by incubating bird. [See also IV B 8 and Nests Above the Ground IX A a(1) 1]

Eastern and central United States south to Florida Keys and Gulf of Mexico (the Nighthawk breeding on the Keys is the Cuban Nighthawk).

Nighthawk

B. Arched Nest

  b(1). Along old fencerows or neglected brushy corner of field

  1. Well hollowed; of dry grasses, straw, leaves, or weed stalks; lined with grass, straw, or bark strips; sometimes an arched passage up to a foot in length is constructed, leading to it.

Gulf of Mexico north through eastern and central United States except northern Minnesota and northern Maine.

Bob-white

b(2). Beneath a tuft of clover, sedge, or grass

1. Of grasses and weeds and lined with finer materials; sometimes with a covered grassy tunnel leading to it. Upon rare occasions the nest has two entrances. Well concealed.

Eastern and central United States (from eastern Minnesota) south to Florida and Gulf of Mexico and west to Nebraska and Kansas.

Meadowlark

b(3). In or under a tussock of grass

1. On ground beneath a tussock of grass or weeds; of grass and usually roughly arched with same material.

Prairies from Canadian border south to central Texas and east to Wisconsin and Illinois.

Western Meadowlark

2. SEE I A a(1) 5 **Grasshopper Sparrow**

II. In Woods

A. Open Nest

a(1). At foot of tree, bush, stump, rock, or log; among roots of fallen tree or where earth has washed away from tree roots on bank

1. SEE Nests Above the Ground VIII A a(3) 4
   American Merganser

2. Of twigs and leaves; lined with moss and grass; well concealed; chiefly in swampy coniferous woods.

   A northern species nesting along northern fringe of eastern and central United States.
   Spruce Grouse

3. Shallow depression in the ground; lined chiefly with dead leaves.

   Eastern United States south to New Jersey and, in Appalachians, to Georgia and Alabama, and central United States south in Mississippi Valley to Michigan, Wisconsin, northeastern Iowa, and locally to Ohio, Indiana, and Missouri.
   Ruffed Grouse

4. A hollow lined with leaves, grass, and a few feathers.

   Prairie brushland and open forests from Canadian border south to western Wisconsin, Minnesota, and central Nebraska.

Sharp-tailed Grouse

5. A large rough structure of leaves, bark strips, grass, moss, and pine needles; lined with grasses, rootlets, feathers, and hair. Sometimes arched over or dome-shaped, the opening being only large enough to admit the bird. [See also B b(1) 2]. In a hole in the ground or in a crevice in bank, in a hole in a log or rocks, among roots of fallen tree, in a tree or stump cavity in woodland or orchard, in a nesting box, or on shelf of building or porch. [See also II B b(1) 2 and Nests Above the Ground VIII A a(3) 21 and IX A a(2) 1]

Southern Massachusetts, Rhode Island, lower Hudson River, Pennsylvania, Ohio, southern Iowa, and southwestern Nebraska south to Florida, Gulf Coast, and Texas.

Carolina Wren

6. Of twigs, grasses, weeds, dead leaves, and sometimes bark strips; lined with fine grasses, rootlets, pine needles, or horsehair; sometimes raised a bit on sprouts or stems, on a dead or sprouting stump, or among rank ferns. [See also Nests Above the Ground VI A a(2) 4 and VIII A a(3) 23]

Eastern and central United States south to central Iowa, northern Indiana, northern Ohio, New Jersey, and, in mountains, to northern Georgia.

Veery

7. Rather bulky; of grasses, rootlets, leaves, and mosses; lined with finer grasses, fern down, hair,

or similar soft material; usually placed in a depression scooped out by the bird. [See also II B b(1) 3]

Eastern and central United States south to northern parts of Gulf States.

Black and White Warbler

8. Bulky; of bark strips, leaves, grass stems, and weeds; lined with bark shreds laid across instead of around the cup, and often with a lining of fine grass stems laid over these; built on a foundation of dry leaves. [See also II A a(3) 6]

Southeastern Minnesota, southern Michigan, and southern New England south to Kansas, Missouri, Delaware, and, in uplands, to Georgia.

Blue-winged Warbler

9. Slight depression in the ground; neat and compact; of strips of soft bark and vegetable fiber; thickly lined with fine dead grass, pine needles, and hair; about 2 inches inside diameter and the same in depth; usually in groves of jack pines with ground cover of blueberry, bearberry, or sweet fern.

North-central part of lower peninsula of Michigan.

Kirtland's Warbler

10. In a cavity in the ground or in a bed of moss, at the base of a stump or tree or alongside a moss-covered log or on side of a bank; of moss, externally like that with which it is usually surrounded; lined with stems of some moss; sometimes bits of leaves, grass, rootlets, and twigs form part of it; carefully concealed; along

wooded watercourses or low-wooded shores of a pond; also in wooded swamps. [See also II A a(6) 1]

Northern Minnesota, northwestern Michigan, northeastern Ohio, New York, northern New England, and, in mountains, to West Virginia.

Northern Water Thrush

11. Bulky; of mud-covered dry leaves, grass, rootlets, and moss; carefully concealed in a shallow cavity in a brook bank where earth has eroded from tree roots or under upturned roots of fallen tree; usually in the wooded valley of a rocky brook or small stream.

Western New England, southeastern Minnesota, and eastern Nebraska south to central South Carolina, northern Georgia, northern Louisiana, and northeastern Texas.

Louisiana Water Thrush

12. Bulky, of dead leaves, grasses, and weed stalks; lined with rootlets or horsehair, or both, sometimes with pine needles; well concealed by surrounding vegetation. May be found in all sorts of unexpected places. [See also II A a(2) 4 and III A a(4) 7]

Gulf States north to southeastern Nebraska, southern Wisconsin, northern Ohio, and lower Hudson Valley (rare).

Kentucky Warbler

13. Of grass, dried leaves, moss, and bark strips; lined with fine rootlets and hairs, and sometimes fern down; usually well concealed. [See also II A a(2) 6 and II A a(3) 7]

Canadian border south to Minnesota, Michigan,

New York, northern New Jersey, and, in mountains, to northern Georgia.

Canada Warbler

14. Of grasses, rootlets, and bark shreds; lined with
finer grasses and rootlets, sometimes with cow
or deer hair.

Northern Minnesota, northern Michigan, Maine,
and, in higher Appalachians, to northern Georgia.

Slate-colored Junco

15. SEE I A a(4) 3 and Nests Above the Ground VI
A a(1) 6   **(Eastern) Field Sparrow**

16. Of coarse grasses, rootlets, and leaves, and
sometimes moss and bark strips; lined with fine
grass or hair; like that of the Song Sparrow,
but larger. [See also II A a(3) 8]

Canadian border south to central Minnesota,
central Wisconsin, northern New England, and in
mountains of Massachusetts, New York, and Pennsylvania.

White-throated Sparrow

a(2). In or under tussocks of grass or weeds
  1. Of grass, weeds, and fibrous roots (seaweed if
  near the coast), and lined with gray down and
  white feathers from female. Also sheltered by
  bushes and sometimes in thick growth of coniferous trees. [See also II A a(3) 1 and II A a(4) 1]

Near lakes, rivers, ponds, and often near sea-
coast. Canadian border south to coast of Maine,
southern New York, central Michigan, Wisconsin,
and central Minnesota.

Red-breasted Merganser

2. Of leaves, bark strips or shreds, fine grasses, and horsehair; lined with crisscross strips and shreds of inner bark and grasses; sometimes unlined, and sometimes the web of the tent caterpillar is used in the construction; usually supported by a base of dead leaves and by weed stalks or small stems of some sprout or brier; rather bulky, but neatly cupped.

Minnesota, New York, and Massachusetts south to Iowa, northern Indiana, northern New Jersey, and, in mountains, to Georgia.

Golden-winged Warbler

3. SEE I A a(1) 2   **Nashville Warbler**

4. SEE II A a(1) 12 and III A a(4) 7

Kentucky Warbler

5. Of weed stalks, some bark strips, grass, and sometimes horsehair; lined with fine black rootlets; sometimes built among shoots springing from a stump.

Canadian border south to central Minnesota, Michigan, New York, and, in mountains, to West Virginia.

Mourning Warbler

6. SEE II A a(1) 13 and II A a(3) 7

Canada Warbler

7. Of leaves, twigs, grass, and bark strips; lined with fine grass, pine needles, or hair; sometimes carelessly made, at other times firm and compact.

Eastern and central United States (except northern Maine) south to Florida and Gulf Coast.

Towhee

8. SEE I A a(1) 7; also Nests Above the Ground
VI A a(2) 7 and VI B b(1) 9   **Song Sparrow**

a(3). In or beneath dense underbrush or shrubbery

1. SEE II A a(2) 1 and II A a(4) 1
Red-breasted Merganser

2. A hollow in the ground; lined with a few
leaves; very well concealed.

Southern woodlands north to Pennsylvania,
eastern Kentucky, and southeastern Missouri.
Turkey

3. Merely a depression in the leaves, with a lining
of a few dead leaves and sometimes a little
dried grass.

Northern Florida and southern Louisiana north
through eastern and central United States.
Woodcock

4. Rather bulky, but neat and compact; of coarse
grass, moss, twigs, or bark; lined with pine
needles, rootlets, or delicate plant fibers.

Canadian border south to central Minnesota,
northern Michigan, Massachusetts, Long Island,
New Jersey, and, in mountains, to Virginia.
(Eastern) Hermit Thrush

5. Of leaves, or leaves and moss, and lined with
moss and sometimes with grasses and horsehair.
Usually sunk in a steep hillside or side of ra-
vine or beside a log in the woods, but sometimes near a swamp or a stream, without much
concealment.

Southwestern Massachusetts, Connecticut, north-

ern Illinois, and southern Iowa south to northern
Georgia and Missouri.

Worm-eating Warbler

6. SEE II A a(1) 8 **Blue-winged Warbler**

7. SEE II A a(1) 13 and II A a(2) 6
Canada Warbler

8. SEE II A a(1) 16 **White-throated Sparrow**

a(4). In woods clear of dense undergrowth
 1. SEE II A a(2) 1 and II A a(3) 1
Red-breasted Merganser

 2. No nest, eggs simply being deposited on dry
 leaves or bare ground, sometimes at the foot
 of a tree; usually in deciduous woods but sometimes in rocky, bushy hillsides. May be slight
 depression about eggs from presence of parent's body during incubation.

 Florida north to southern Maryland, southern
 Ohio, southern Indiana, and southeastern Kansas.
Chuck-will's-widow

 3. Adds no nesting material, simply placing eggs
 on leafy forest floor in mixed growth of oak,
 beech, and pine, either on open ground or under shadow of branches of small bush. May be
 slight depression about eggs from presence of
 parent's body during incubation.

 Eastern and central United States south to
 northern Georgia and northern Louisiana.
(Eastern) Whip-poor-will

 4. Of fine grasses, arranged in a neat symmetrical
 manner. In the northern part of bird's range

the nest is domed. [See also II B b(2) 2]. In open pine woods.

Florida, Gulf Coast, and Texas north to Maryland, southwestern Pennsylvania, southern Ohio, central Illinois, and southeastern Iowa.

Pine Woods Sparrow

a(5). Among rocks or in hollow logs

1. No nesting material, eggs being deposited on the ground, or ledge of rocks, in caves, hollow logs and stumps, or hollow stubs. Usually in a secluded place. [See also Nests Above the Ground VIII A a(3) 5]

Gulf of Mexico north to western Connecticut, western New York, and northern Minnesota.

Turkey Vulture

a(6). In swampy woods

1. SEE II A a(1) 10   **Northern Water Thrush**

2. On the ground in tamarack swamps; compactly built, sunk in moss, and composed entirely of dried grass in some instances, built of shreds of bark, leaf stems, and grass in other cases; lined with fine rootlets and hair.

Northern and central Minnesota and northern Michigan.

Connecticut Warbler

B. Arched Nest

b(1). At foot of tree, bush, stump, rock, or log; among roots of fallen tree, etc.

1. Of twigs, leaves, and moss; lined with fine rootlets, feathers, fur, or hair, with a small

circular opening in one side only, just large enough to admit the little owner. May be built in cavity of low stump or tree. [See also Nests Above the Ground VIII A a(3) 19]

Minnesota, New York, and, in mountains, to North Carolina.

Winter Wren

2. SEE II A a(1) 5 and Nests Above the Ground VIII A a(3) 21 and IX A a(2) 1 **Carolina Wren**

3. SEE II A a(1) 7 **Black and White Warbler**

b(2). Among dead leaves of forest floor

1. Bulky; of grass or sedge, dry leaves, and bark strips; lined with hair, fine grasses, or pine needles; usually sunk somewhat and roofed over with an arch of leaves and grass, giving it the form of an old-fashioned brick oven; entrance at one side; usually concealed by overhanging plants or the leaves of shrubs.

Eastern and central United States south to eastern North Carolina, northern Georgia, Arkansas, and Kansas.

Ovenbird

2. In a depression in the ground; of dry grasses and lined with fine grass tops; cylindrical in shape, about 7 or 8 inches long by 3 inches high and 4½ inches wide; opening well hidden in side and usually faces west. [See also II A a(4) 4]

Florida, Gulf Coast, and Texas north to Maryland, southwestern Pennsylvania, southern Ohio, central Illinois, and southeastern Iowa.

Pine Woods Sparrow

III. In Marshes

A. Open Nest

a(1). In or among reeds, flags, rushes, or sedges

1. Of marsh grass, reeds, and rushes, usually attached to surrounding vegetation but sometimes found floating.

> Western Minnesota and North Dakota.
>
> **Holboell's Grebe**

2. A mass of water-soaked, decaying vegetation floating among rushes in a slough, generally attached to its surroundings.

> Lakes of Maine, Minnesota, and northern Nebraska.
>
> **Horned Grebe**

3. A floating matted structure of reeds and sedges, with a slight depression in the center; usually lightly fastened to the living reeds so that it will move up and down but not be carried away from its position.

> Dakotas, Nebraska, and western Minnesota.
>
> **Western Grebe**

4. Floating structure of partially decayed reeds or flags, bent or matted down, with perhaps some coarse sedgy grass, most of nest material below

surface of the water; sometimes built up from bottom in shallow water, of water-soaked, decaying vegetation.

Gulf States north through eastern and central United States.

Pied-billed Grebe

5. In dense cattail marshes; partially concealed by new flags growing among tall dead flags of previous season's growth. A practically flat platform of dead flags, a foot or more in diameter, raised above water or mud only a few inches. Occasionally flags are arched over nest. Nests also found in meadows over almost dry ground.

Gulf of Mexico north through eastern and central United States.

American Bittern

6. A flimsy platform of flags, reeds, and grasses, slightly hollowed, on foundation of flags bent down and interlaced, from a few inches to 4 or 5 feet above the water. Tops of growing flags may also be interlaced over nest. Usual size: 4 or 5 inches deep by 6 or 7 inches across. [See also Nests Above the Ground I A 1]

Gulf of Mexico north through eastern and central United States to southern Maine and Minnesota.

(Eastern) Least Bittern

7. Well made, bulky and deep, of reeds or flags; lined with whitish down; frequently covered with a downy blanket and sometimes canopied

with rushes. [See also III B b(1) 1]. In cattail swamps or near shallow, marsh-bordered lakes.

Canadian border south to central Nebraska, southern Wisconsin, and southeastern Michigan.

Redhead

8. Bulky, of dry grass and reeds; lined with down; usually in tall rushes or reeds near water.

Dakotas, Nebraska, Minnesota, and occasionally southern Wisconsin.

Canvas-back

9. A bulky, buoyant structure, often basketlike, in reeds and sometimes floating on water; of dry reeds, rushes, and grass and lined with down. Often the canopying rushes are bent over by the bird. Usually near water, generally in marshes, but frequently on the shores of lakes and ponds; sometimes nest is built on the ground. [See also III B b(1) 2]

Canadian border south to Nebraska, northern Illinois, and southeastern Michigan.

Ruddy Duck

10. Well constructed; of flags and grasses held a few inches above the water by surrounding cattail flags. Outside diameter, 6 inches; inside, 3 inches in diameter by 2 inches deep. May have canopy of flags and runway leading to it.

Eastern and central United States south to Maryland, southern Ohio, northern Missouri, and Kansas.

Sora

11. Slightly hollowed heap of reeds, grass, or flags; lined with grass; among clumps of tall water

plants; usually on buoyant platform of broken-down flags, a few inches above the water, but sometimes on the ground. External diameter, 15 to 20 inches; egg cavity, 7 inches across and 2 to 2½ inches deep.

Gulf of Mexico north to Vermont, New York, Minnesota, and Nebraska.

Florida Gallinule

12. A floating structure among reeds; of dead reeds, grasses, and bits of decayed vegetation; often in colonies.

Northern edge of central and eastern United States south to Arkansas, Tennessee, and New Jersey; casually to Florida.

Coot

13. See IV A 3 **Black-necked Stilt**

14. Of dead rushes; among standing rushes and grass of marshes bordering lakes and rivers; often floating.

North and South Dakota and southeastern Minnesota.

Franklin's Gull

15. A mere hollow in piles of reeds or a well-made structure in heap of vegetation; sometimes buoyed up by dead reeds or flags in several feet of water. Occasionally the nest is a mere hollow on muddy shore. [See also IV A 8]. Breeds in colonies.

Salt marshes scattered along coast from Maryland to Texas, and in western prairie marshes east to Minnesota and northeastern Illinois.

Forster's Tern

16. Usually a careless structure of a few dead sedges
and grass but sometimes well built; at times a
mere hollow in a pile of floating rubbish or old
muskrat house. Occasionally nest might be
found on bit of driftwood or piece of board.

Canadian border south to Missouri and Tennessee and east to western Pennsylvania, central New
York, and northern Vermont.

Black Tern

a(2). In weeds or grass
1. Beautifully built of grass and lined with fine
grass and little down; in a hummock about 6
inches above the ground and in an opening
about 4 to 5 feet square.

Marshes and rice fields of Texas and Louisiana.
Fulvous Tree Duck

2. Of reeds, flags, grasses, and leaves; warmly
lined with down from female's breast. Usually
near water, but sometimes far from it, and
commonly hidden by reeds, flags, leaves, and
low branches. Generally in a marsh but sometimes on dry cultivated ground. [See also I A
a(1) 1]

Canadian border south to southern Texas, southern Kansas, southern Missouri, southeastern Illinois, southwestern Indiana, southern Ohio, and
northern Ohio.

Mallard

3. Large, neatly constructed; of weeds, grass, flags,
and leaves; lined with duck down and breast or
flank feathers (dusky with central buffy streak
or buffy edgings). Average size: inside diame-

ter, 8 inches; outside diameter, 18 inches; depth, 2 inches.

Eastern states, Maine south to North Carolina, and west to northern Illinois, Wisconsin, and Minnesota.

Black Duck

4. Of grasses and leaves and rimmed with down. On dry ground.

Florida and coastal belt of Louisiana and Texas.
Mottled Duck

5. On the ground in marsh grass or rushes; of grass and leaves and lined with dark-gray down, sometimes thickly lined; breast feathers are frequently mixed with the down. In wet places such as marshy borders of shallow lakes or wet meadows.

Canadian border south to northern Nebraska and northern Iowa and locally east to western Pennsylvania and Maine.

Ring-necked Duck

6. Usually a slight affair and little hollowed (an inch or two thick) on dry ground, but bulky, high, and deeply hollowed if on wet ground, when it may be raised on a platform of sticks to a height of 15 to 18 inches; of dry grass, stubble, and weed stalks and lined with finer material of the same character. Inside diameter, 8 to 9 inches; outside diameter, 20 to 30 inches.

Gulf of Mexico north to northeastern United States.

Marsh Hawk

7. Of grasses, weeds, and roots, usually on a slight knoll or grassy flat, often on a platform of dead vegetation in shallow water; sometimes bulky. Frequently it is a mere depression in the ground and lined with dry grass and weed stems. [See also III A a(3) 7]

> Minnesota, Michigan, Wisconsin, and Dakotas; also in Florida and southern Georgia.

Sandhill Crane

8. Of weeds and grasses; deeply hollowed and lined with grasses; well concealed by interlacing of surrounding grass. About 8 inches in diameter and placed 6 inches to a foot above water.

> Gulf of Mexico north to Massachusetts, New York, and southern Minnesota, and west to Kansas.

King Rail

9. Slightly hollowed and rather compactly constructed; of weeds, coarse grasses, and dead stalks; lined with chips of cattail blades; well concealed; sometimes placed on a pile of broken-down reeds or drift. Usually in drier location than Sora.

> Eastern and central United States south to Nebraska, Missouri, Kentucky, and eastern North Carolina.

Virginia Rail

10. Of finest grasses; over shallow water or wet ground; 1 inch thick, 4 to 5 inches in diameter. An erratic "mystery" bird, inhabiting a local-

ity for one season, then perhaps not appearing the following season or for several years.

Locally in northern parts of eastern and central United States.

Yellow Rail

11. SEE I A a(4) 1   **Palm Warbler**

12. Coarsely built; of dried grass or seaweed; lined with fine grass or similar material; in a tussock of grass or in grass; sometimes placed among driftwood or dry seaweed just above high-water mark of summer tides.

Along coast from Virginia north; also inland prairie marshes of Minnesota and the Dakotas.

Sharp-tailed Sparrow

13. In areas of fine grass in salt marshes, over water, or in drift above high-water mark; of dried grasses; lined with fine grass.

Salt marshes along coast from southern Massachusetts to Florida and along Gulf to Texas.

Seaside Sparrow

14. Composed of dry salt-marsh grass and lined with very fine grass; attached to some upright marsh grass.

Coastal prairie near Cape Sable, Florida (an area about 6 miles in length and not more than $\frac{1}{2}$ mile in width).

Cape Sable Seaside Sparrow

15. Of grass and a few leaves; lined with similar materials; sometimes arched over with grasses or sedges. [See also III B b(1) 7]

Eastern and central United States south to New

Jersey, West Virginia, northern Missouri, and
northern Nebraska.

Swamp Sparrow

a(3). In the ground

1. SEE IV B 1   **Common Loon**

2. A slight hollow among grass, padded with
   grasses and weed stems and lined with down;
   usually near water. Sometimes built in a
   meadow. [See also I A a(5) 1]

   Canadian border south to Kansas, northern
   Iowa, and southern Wisconsin, and locally east
   to western Pennsylvania and coastal Delaware and
   North Carolina.

   Gadwall

3. Usually in a hollow on dry ground in or near
   a marsh, in dense growth of grass, sometimes
   under bushes. [See also III A a(4) 1]. Of grass,
   sedges, weeds, feathers, and much down.

   Dakotas, northern Nebraska, southern Minnesota, and northern Michigan.

   Green-winged Teal

4. A hollow in long, thick grass near water, filled
   with well-built nest of fine grass mixed with
   down and lined with down and breast feathers
   of duck (brown to drab with large whitish centers). More down added as incubation advances.

   Canadian border south to Kansas, Missouri, Illinois, Ohio, and New Jersey.

   Blue-winged Teal

5. A slight hollow, lined with grasses and weeds and an abundance of gray down. A neat well-built structure for a duck. Usually in dry ground and either concealed or open, sometimes rather distant from water.

North Dakota, Minnesota, Wisconsin, Michigan, south to northern Nebraska and northern Indiana.
Baldpate

6. A hollow, usually hidden in grass or under bushes. [See also III A a(4) 2]. Lined with grasses and rimmed with down, the eggs often covered (as incubation advances) with it. Sometimes a hollow in dry ground in a field. [See also I A a(5) 3]

Canadian border south to Nebraska and western Iowa and locally east to western Pennsylvania.
Shoveller

7. SEE III A a(2) 7   **Sandhill Crane**

8. A depression in grass or moss, lined with a little grass; sometimes a very slight affair of straw and leaves is made and raised above the surrounding surface. Size: 6 inches, outside diameter; 3 inches, inside diameter.

Eastern and central United States south to northwestern Pennsylvania, northern Illinois, and South Dakota.
Wilson's Snipe

9. A mere depression in the ground lined with a little grass; in fresh or salt water marshes; sometimes a carelessly built structure of small

reeds and grass placed in a tussock of grass or weeds, close to the water. [See also III A a(4) 5]

Mainly along Atlantic Coast from Delaware Bay to Texas and in prairies south to Iowa and Nebraska.

Willet

10. On the ground or sunk in it, usually among bushes, such as alders or smaller shrubs and well concealed by swamp grass; of grass; lined with finer grass and a few hairs; cup-shaped.

Minnesota, New Hampshire, and Maine.

Wilson's Warbler

a(4). Beneath bushes or grass clumps

1. SEE III A a(3) 3   **Green-winged Teal**

2. SEE III A a(3) 6 and I A a(5) 3   **Shoveller**

3. No nesting material, eggs being deposited on the ground, under logs or bushes, or in hollow logs or hollows of decaying stumps or trees, sometimes in caves or cavities in rocks. On islands or dry spots in swamps or marshes. [See also III A a(6) 1]

Gulf states north to Maryland, West Virginia, southern Ohio, southern Indiana, and Missouri.

Black Vulture

4. Of grass, leaves, dead vines, moss, and other old vegetation; near water. Sometimes a short distance above ground in a maze of vines or thick bushes. [See also Nests Above the Ground VI A a(2) 1]

In swamps and marshes of Florida and southern Georgia.

Limpkin

5. SEE III A a(3) 9 **Willet**

6. A slight depression or hollow in ground, of matted vegetation, lined with scanty dried vegetation and some owl feathers.

 Eastern and central United States south to New Jersey, northern Ohio, and southern Kansas.
 Short-eared Owl

7. SEE II A a(1) 12 and II A a(2) 4
 Kentucky Warbler

8. Rather large and bulky, deep and cup-shaped; of coarse grass, dried leaves, and bark strips; lined with finer grasses, tendrils, rootlets, and sometimes hairs. [See also III B b(1) 6]

 Eastern and central United States south to Florida and Gulf Coast.
 Yellow-throat

9. Cup-shaped and deep; of fine grass, carefully concealed in the center of a thick tuft of grass.

 In prairie marshes of North Dakota, Minnesota, and northwestern Michigan.
 Leconte's Sparrow

10. Of grasses, lined with fine blades of the same material.

 Along northern fringe of eastern and central United States.
 Lincoln's Sparrow

a(5). In moss or under a stump or upturned root
 1. Cup-shaped, usually imbedded in moss, built of sphagnum or other moss; lined with fine

grasses and fine black rootlets and pine needles. In secluded mossy swamps, wooded with coniferous trees.

Along northern fringe of United States (northern Michigan, southern Minnesota, Maine) and in southern New Hampshire and rarely to Pennsylvania.

Yellow-bellied Flycatcher

a(6). Among rocks and in hollow logs
    1. SEE III A a(4) 3   **Black Vulture**

B. Arched Nest

  b(1). Beneath bushes or in clumps of grass
    1. SEE III A a(1) 7   **Redhead**

    2. SEE III A a(1) 9   **Ruddy Duck**

    3. On the ground under drift trash or in tussocks; of dead reeds and grass, and well concealed from above by an interlacing of surrounding grass to provide a canopy.

      Salt marshes along Atlantic Coast and Gulf Coast from Connecticut to Texas.

Clapper Rail

    4. Placed in grass that may be 8 to 10 inches high; of fine grasses, with covering of standing grasses woven over it to provide canopy and entrance from the side. Resembles nest of Meadowlark, though smaller. Inside: diameter, 3+ inches; depth, $2\frac{1}{2}$ inches. Outside: diameter, $3\frac{1}{2}$ inches;

depth, 4½ inches. May be built as open, rather than arched, nest.

Along coast from Florida to Massachusetts and locally inland to Iowa and Kansas.

Black Rail

5. A mere hollow in the ground or sometimes a collection of grasses or sedges, lined with a little grass, and usually concealed by overhanging grass or other vegetation, which may be drawn together by bird; sometimes in grassland.

Canadian border south to Nebraska, Iowa, and northwestern Indiana.

Wilson's Phalarope

6. SEE III A a(4) 8   **Yellow-throat**

7. SEE III A a(2) 15   **Swamp Sparrow**

IV. On or Near Seashore and Lake Beaches

A. Nesting in Colonies

1. Of sticks, coarse grass, and weed stalks, and lined with finer grasses; usually on an island in lake or lagoon. Sometimes nest is built in low bushes, frequently in mangrove growth. Also at times on the ground. [See also Nests Above the Ground VII B b(3) 1]

     Along the Atlantic and Gulf Coasts from North Carolina to Texas.

     (Eastern) Brown Pelican

2. Of mosses, seaweed, sticks, or grass and lined with gray down from breast of bird, the lining being added gradually during the month of incubation; usually sheltered by rocks, trees, undergrowth, or grasses.

     Principally on coastal islands along Maine coast.

     Common Eider

3. A mere hollow lined with grasses, on dry ground near water; in small colonies. Sometimes a frail structure of grass and small stems among grasses, reeds, and rushes, in shallow water and built up from 4 to 7 inches. [See also III A a(1) 13]

     Florida, coastal South Carolina, and coast of Louisiana and Texas.

     Black-necked Stilt

4. Large and bulky; of dry grasses and well-cupped; usually on small island.

>   Along coast, Maine to Long Island (rarely).
>   **Great Black-backed Gull**

5. Of eelgrass or other seaweeds, but often of marsh grasses, weeds, sticks, chips, and sometimes a few feathers, shells, and tree mosses (Climacium spp.); sometimes placed on rocks or cliffs [See also VI A 2], and sometimes in thick vegetation.

>   Along coast, Maine to Long Island; also about larger lakes of Canadian border.
>   **Herring Gull**

6. Rather well built; of grasses, seaweed, and sticks, more or less concealed among thick low vegetation; sometimes a mere hollow in sand without concealment.

>   Grassy islands or in salt marshes along the coast from Maine to Texas.
>   **Laughing Gull**

7. A mere depression in the sand or, if placed among grasses, a pile of sedges or grasses; sometimes lined with shells. [See also IV B 7]. Occasionally found in colonies of other terns.

>   Locally along coast from Maryland to Texas.
>   **Gull-billed Tern**

8. A mere hollow on muddy shore. [See also III A a(1) 15]

>   Salt marshes scattered along coast from Maryland

to Texas, and in western prairie marshes east to Minnesota and northeastern Illinois.

Forster's Tern

9. Usually a mere depression in the beach sand or pebbles, lined with a few bits of shell or small stones; sometimes a well-built mound of grasses and seaweeds; sometimes of fishbones; and other times a hollow in stranded eelgrass.

Locally on sandy beaches and small islands from Canadian border south to Gulf of Mexico.

Common Tern

10. Similar to that of the Common Tern, but usually with less nesting material.

Coastal islands of Maine and Massachusetts.

Arctic Tern

11. A mere hollow in bare sand; often lined with grass or seaweed; sometimes placed among beach grass and other vegetation.

Scattered localities along Atlantic and Gulf Coasts from Maine to Texas; most common near eastern Long Island and southern New England. A small colony on Dry Tortugas, Florida.

Roseate Tern

12. Slight attempt at nest, the eggs being dropped in a "scoop" on the sandy beach.

On Dry Tortugas, Florida.

Sooty Tern

13. Slight hollow in sand.

Coastal from Texas to Massachusetts; also in Mississippi and Missouri River systems north to Ohio, Iowa, southwestern Kansas, and Nebraska.

Least Tern

14. Slight hollow in sand.

> Along coast from Virginia to Texas.
>
> **Royal Tern**

15. Mere hollow in sand; sometimes not even a hollow is excavated, the eggs being merely deposited on the sand. Often nests in company with Royal Terns.

> Locally along coast from North Carolina to Texas.
>
> **Cabot's Tern**

16. A mere hollow scooped in dry sand.

> Along Gulf of Mexico and locally on Great Lakes.
>
> **Caspian Tern**

17. A slight hollow in sand, pebbles, or shells of beach; on higher salt flats and shell ridges.

> Along coast from Texas to Long Island and occasionally Massachusetts.
>
> **Black Skimmer**

18. Merely a burrow in the soil, sometimes under rock or in crevice. [See also VI A 4]

> On islands along coast of Maine.
>
> **Atlantic Puffin**

B. Nesting Singly

1. Usually a mere hollow in the sand, within a few feet of water and usually without nesting material but sometimes a rough nest is constructed of sticks and reeds; occasionally the top of an old muskrat house is utilized and at times the nest may consist of a mass of reeds

and other vegetation on edge of marsh. [See also III A a(3) 1]

About shores of inland lakes on northern edge of eastern and central United States.

Common Loon

2. SEE III A a(1) 9 and III B b(1) 2   **Ruddy Duck**

3. A hollow or slight depression in the sand; often decorated with a few bits of shells.

Locally along coast from Virginia to Texas.

American Oyster Catcher

4. Slight hollow in sand; sometimes lined with pebbles and bits of shell and driftwood; may be placed at base of a low sand dune.

Along coast, Maine south to North Carolina and locally inland to Pennsylvania, northern Ohio, northeastern Illinois, and Nebraska.

Piping Plover

5. Slight hollow in sand.

Along Gulf Coast from Florida to Texas.

(Cuban) Snowy Plover

6. A slight depression in sandy beach just above high-water mark; often encircled with broken bits of shells.

Coastal islands from Virginia to Texas.

Wilson's Plover

7. SEE IV A 7   **Gull-billed Tern**

8. SEE I A a(6) 1 and Nests Above the Ground IX A a(1) 1   **Nighthawk**

V. In Burrows in the Ground

A. Nesting in Colonies

1. A slight collection of pebbles, short grasses, weeds, rootlets, and perhaps a few feathers, usually at the end of a burrow; the burrows, like ratholes and only a few inches in diameter, usually from 1 to 3 feet long, extend downward then run along nearly horizontally not many inches below the surface and into a roundish chamber at end, slightly enlarged; or the burrow may be a short one under a rock.

   Sea islands off Maine and Massachusetts.
   Leach's Petrel

2. In a chamber about 5 inches in diameter, at the end of a tunnel in bank measuring from 15 inches to 8 feet or more, is placed a flimsy nest of straw, grass, weed stalks, and rootlets, lined with feathers.

   Eastern and central United States south to Virginia, northern Alabama, Louisiana, and Texas.
   Bank Swallow

B. Nesting Singly

1. A collection of weed stalks, dried broken bits of horse or cow dung, bits of skin, or any convenient material, placed in an enlarged chamber from 5 to 10 feet from entrance of abandoned prairie-dog, skunk, fox, or badger

burrow. Sometimes digs own burrow if soil is not too hard.

Minnesota, western Iowa, and Louisiana; also prairies of central and southern Florida.

Burrowing Owl

2. In a hole, about 4 inches in diameter, excavated in a sandy, clay, or gravelly bank, preferably near water, the hole running in nearly horizontally from 3 to 15 feet (usually about 4 or 5 feet). Often straight or nearly so, sometimes with turn near inner end; "nest" an enlargement at inner end of excavation, usually of bits of clean white fishbones, fish scales, or fragments of shells of crustaceans, probably the remains of ejected pellets; sometimes of leaves, sticks, and grasses.

Eastern and central United States south to Gulf of Mexico.

(Eastern) Belted Kingfisher

3. Large, bulky, loosely constructed; in burrow, usually in precipitous banks of clay, sand, or gravel near water; of sticks, roots, straw, weed stalks, grass, and leaves; lined with grasses, rootlets, bits of dead leaves, pine needles, and sometimes feathers; sometimes built on bridge supports or wall along water.

Gulf of Mexico north to Massachusetts, New York, Minnesota, and North Dakota.

Rough-winged Swallow

VI. On Rocks or Rocky Ledges

A. On Ledges of Rocks on Islands off Coast

1. A platform rather loosely put together, but sometimes well built; of sticks and weed stalks or sticks and seaweed; sometimes nests on ground or in low trees and bushes. [See also Nests Above the Ground VII B b(3) 2]

    Locally throughout eastern and central United States south to Florida and Gulf of Mexico.
    Double-crested Cormorant

2. SEE IV A 5   **Herring Gull**

3. Eggs merely laid in a crevice, rift, or fissure in cliff or sea ledge, or under some rock or among loose rocks. Sometimes the eggs are laid so far back under or among the rocks as to be inaccessible.

    On islands and shore cliffs along coast of Maine.
    Black Guillemot

4. A burrow in the fissures of rocks. [See also IV A 18]

    On islands along coast of Maine.
    Atlantic Puffin

B. On Rocky Ledge of Cliff

1. SEE Nests Above the Ground VII B b(1) 7
    Swainson's Hawk

2. Sometimes in a tall tree on a mountainside and sometimes relatively low in a tree in rather open country but usually on inaccessible cliffs, on a shelf of rock or earth, or high bank of lake or stream; a bulky structure of sticks, lined with hay, twigs, or green grass; if used for many years becomes moist and in part decayed. [See also Nests Above the Ground VII A 3]

Locally in Appalachians from Canadian border to Southern States.

Golden Eagle

3. A slight hollow, $1\frac{1}{2}$ inches deep and a foot wide, scraped in accumulated soil and rubbish, sometimes lined with grass and surrounded by flakes of rock, a few twigs, bones of birds, and pellets.

Locally throughout eastern and central United States south to northern Georgia and Louisiana

Duck Hawk

4. SEE Nests Above the Ground VII B b(1) 9 and VIII A a(3) 6   **(Eastern) Pigeon Hawk**

5. SEE Nests Above the Ground VII A 7   **Raven**

Nests Above the Ground

I. Hanging or Semihanging

A. Attached to Reeds or Bushes in Marshes

1. SEE Nests On or In the Ground III A a(1) 6
   (Eastern) Least Bittern

2. Cup-shaped and well built; of dead reeds and plant stems in low bushes.

   Locally in peninsular Florida.
   Eastern Glossy Ibis

3. Cup-shaped; well and compactly built; of dead reeds attached to upright stalks of living ones.

   Southern Texas and southern Louisiana; occasional in Florida.
   White-faced Glossy Ibis

4. A platform of rushes, like a shallow basket, suspended among and woven into the vegetation.

   Lowland swamps from Florida and Texas north to South Carolina and Tennessee.
   Purple Gallinule

5. Coconut-shaped or spherical; of grasses and reed stalks; lined with finer grasses, cattail down and feathers; entrance on side and sometimes plastered with mud; usually in cattail marshes.

   Massachusetts, northern Vermont, Great Lakes, North Dakota south to Florida and Gulf Coast.
   Long-billed Marsh Wren

6. Spherical; of grasses; lined with plant down; without mud; in wet grassy meadows.

   Eastern and central United States (except northern Maine) south to northern Delaware, Indiana, Missouri, and eastern Kansas.

   Short-billed Marsh Wren

7. Usually built among canes but sometimes in small bushes, generally in swampy locations but occasionally in bushes in high land some distance from water. A bulky and inartistic affair of water-soaked leaves (sweet gum, water oak, pepperidge, or holly), lined with fine pine needles and moss.

   In wooded swamps from Maryland, southern Virginia, southern Indiana, Oklahoma south to northern Florida and Louisiana.

   Swainson's Warbler

8. Cup-shaped, of cane leaves, lined with dry weeds and rootlets or, in southern swamps, with the dead inner fibers of Tillandsia. [See also I C c(1) d(1) 11]

   Rhode Island, central New York, southern Michigan, northern Iowa, northeastern Nebraska south to northern Florida and Gulf of Mexico.

   Hooded Warbler

9. Bulky, rather compact, thick-edged, of blades of grass and sedge; lined with finer blades; from 1 to 3 feet above water. Attached to cattail flags, reeds, and wild rice.

   Canadian border south and east locally to Nebraska, Iowa, southern Wisconsin, and northern Indiana.

   Yellow-headed Blackbird

10. Bowl-shaped, rather bulky; of grasses and weed stalks; lined with finer grass and rootlets; deeply hollowed.

   Eastern and central United States south to Florida and Gulf of Mexico.

   Red-wing

11. Of fine grass stems; from 4 to 16 inches above the ground, not arched, but usually concealed from view by wisps of grass carelessly arranged as if for protection from the sun.

   Salt marshes around Merritt Island in vicinity of Titusville, Florida.

   Dusky Seaside Sparrow

B. Attached to Bushes in Wet Meadows or Swampy Thickets

1. Usually in mangrove thickets in the South but also in bushes or even trees and in reeds or tangles of southern swamps or marshes; usually of mangrove twigs but also of reed stalks and weeds. [See also VII B b(3) 13]

   Low country from South Carolina to Texas.

   White Ibis

2. Cup-shaped, compact, somewhat loosely finished, even ragged appearance outside and below; of bark, grasses, vegetable fibers, and weed stalks; lined with finer grasses, hair, or plant down; in upright crotch of small bush, sometimes wild rose, 2 to 4 feet above the ground.

   Eastern and central United States south to central Arkansas, Kentucky, northern New Jersey, and Connecticut, and, in mountains, to West Virginia.

   Alder Flycatcher

3. Cup-shaped, attached by brim and suspended from forked twigs in trees and bushes; from 5 to 20 feet above ground; of dry grasses, shreds of bark, cotton, lichens, and spiders' webs; the lining being soft cottonlike fibers; the walls neatly and firmly interwoven.

In mangroves in southern Florida (Keys, southern tip, and southern coast to Tampa Bay).

Black-whiskered Vireo

4. Of fine grasses and leaves; 1 to 3 feet from the ground. Cypress swamps and river bottoms. (Perhaps the rarest song bird in North America today.)

Southeastern Missouri, northeastern Arkansas, western Kentucky, northern Alabama, and South Carolina.

Bachman's Warbler

C. Attached to Upland Trees and Bushes

c(1). Fully suspended

d(1). Less than 2 inches deep inside

1. In forks of elm and oak within 6 feet of the ground; a perfectly woven structure of bark strips, grasses, skeleton leaves, spiders' webs, and caterpillar silk.

Central Texas, Oklahoma, and southern Kansas.

Black-capped Vireo

2. In forks of bushes in wettish thickets; cup-shaped; of bits of wood, bark strips, grasses, mosses, lichens, and plant fibers; decorated exteriorly with spiders' nests, bits of rotten wood, newspaper, and rags.

Florida and Gulf of Mexico north to Massa-

chusetts, New York, Ohio, and southern Wisconsin.
White-eyed Vireo

3. In forked twigs of a bush or small tree. Neat,
   cup-shaped structure, compact and smooth; of
   fine bark strips, plant fibers, and leaves, and
   lined with fine grass, rootlets, hair, and down.
   In willows and bushes along streams.

   Texas north to northwestern Indiana, northern
   Illinois, and southern South Dakota.
   Bell's Vireo

4. In middle forks of deciduous (or at times coniferous) trees. Cup-shaped; of bark strips and
   plant fibers; lined with finer grasses; beautifully adorned with lichens and cocoons held
   in place with caterpillars' silk and spiders'
   webs; often placed in an oak tree.

   Eastern and central United States (except north-
   ern Maine) south to northern Florida and Gulf
   Coast.
   Yellow-throated Vireo

5. In terminal forks of evergreens (usually). Cup-
   shaped; usually decorated externally with
   birch-bark strips, oak catkins, or with leaves,
   lichens, and plant down, and often lined with
   pine needles; suspended by vegetable strings,
   hair, cobwebs, and cocoon silk.

   Canadian border south to Minnesota, Michigan,
   northern New Jersey, and, in Appalachians, to
   northern Georgia.
   Blue-headed Vireo

6. In forks of saplings or low branches of tall
   trees. Cup-shaped; durable; of bark strips, bits

of dead wood, paper, and plant down; lined with finer strips of bark, vine tendrils, and sometimes pine needles; ornamented with cocoons and bits of wasps' and spiders' nests.

Eastern and central United States south to central Florida and Gulf Coast.

Red-eyed Vireo

7. In forks of tall shrubs or trees. Cup-shaped; of shreds of bark, weed stems, and shreds of usnea; decorated externally with thin strips of birch bark, seed tufts of willows; lined with pine needles and fine grass; usually found in willows, poplars, and alders of second-growth woods about the edges of farm lands.

Along the northern fringe of eastern and central United States.

Philadelphia Vireo

8. In end forks in the upper part of large deciduous trees. Cup-shaped; of grasses and plant fibers; lined with finer grasses and hair; lacks exterior ornamentation of other vireos' nests.

Eastern and central United States south to North Carolina, southern Louisiana, and northwestern Texas.

(Eastern) Warbling Vireo

9. Near the end of branches of (preferably) coniferous, but also of deciduous, trees. Gourd-shaped, hollowed out of usnea, with entrance hole on side and lined with grass or hair; from 5 to 30 feet above ground. Rarely built on a branch among twigs and covered with usnea

brought for the purpose. In humid woodlands where usnea or Spanish moss hangs from trees.

Eastern and central United States south to Florida, Gulf Coast, and Texas.

Parula Warbler

10. In forks of small branches of deciduous trees; cup-shaped, rather shallow; of weed stems, fine grass, bark strips, and plant fibers, securely bound together with spiders' webs and decorated with bits of lichens; lined with hair, dead grass, bark strips; from 20 to 90 feet from the ground. [See also II B 2]

Central New York, Ohio, southern Michigan, southeastern Minnesota, and southeastern Nebraska south to northern parts of Gulf States, chiefly west of the Appalachians.

Cerulean Warbler

11. Cup-shaped, generally compactly built with a well-woven rim; of leaves, bark strips, weeds, and plant down; lined with fine rootlets, mosses, grasses, pine needles, and horsehair; in bush or sapling 1 to 5 feet above the ground; in bushy borders of upland woods or in hillside thickets. At the northern limit of range laurel is frequently selected; at southern limit, canes. [See also I A 8]

Rhode Island, central New York, southern Michigan, northern Iowa, and southern Nebraska south to northern Florida and Gulf of Mexico.

Hooded Warbler

d(2). Over 2 inches deep inside

1. At extreme ends of drooping branches in such trees as large elms or near the trunk in smaller

maples or other trees. Gourd-shaped, bulging
at the bottom, and normally gray-colored; of
plant fibers, string, yarn, grasses, hair, and
bark.

Eastern and central United States south to northern Georgia, Louisiana, and southern Texas (absent in southeastern coastal plain).

Baltimore Oriole

c(2). Partly suspended
    d(1). Less than 2 inches deep inside
        1. On a low, rather horizontal or drooping
branch, usually in a fork toward the end of
a sapling generally on a bank; from 5 to 20 feet
high; of rootlets, grasses, mosses, weed stems,
or similar materials, usually decorated with
catkins from some tree, and sometimes with
blossoms. Structure not as neat, deep, or well
built as those of other small flycatchers, with
little lining and thin bottom; often resembles
a bunch of "drift" left in crotch of a low
branch by the high water of the stream which
it often overhangs. In well-watered woodlands
and thickets.

Florida and Gulf of Mexico north to Nebraska,
Iowa, southern Michigan, Lake Erie, western New
York, and southern New England.

Acadian Flycatcher

        2. In coniferous trees. Globular, with small open-
ing at top; of green mosses, usnea and other
lichens, soft fine bark strips, bits of leaves and
rootlets, and lined with feathers. Usually well
concealed by foliage.

Minnesota, Michigan, New York, and, in mountains, to North Carolina.

(Eastern) Golden-crowned Kinglet

d(2). Over 2 inches deep inside

  1. On small branches of fruit (and sometimes of shade) trees. Basket-shaped; of grass. When new, difficult of detection in the foliage.

       Gulf of Mexico north to Massachusetts, central New York, Ohio, Michigan, northwestern Minnesota, and North Dakota.

                      Orchard Oriole

II. Covered on Outside with Lichens and Saddled on Branch

A. Less than 2 Inches, Outside Diameter

1. Cup-shaped, very small; of plant down, fastened to limbs and branches with spiders' or caterpillars' webs and covered so perfectly with lichens as to appear a protuberance on the limb; usually placed on a small, down-sloping branch. Average size: outside diameter, $1\frac{1}{2}$ inches; outside depth, $1\frac{1}{4}$ inches.

   Eastern and central United States south to Gulf of Mexico.

   Ruby-throated Hummingbird

2. Cup-shaped, gracefully contracted at brim; composed of soft, silky milkweed or cattail down, withered blossoms, or other dainty material, pinned together with fine grasses, old leaf stems, and horsehair; exterior decorated with lichens, held by spiders' webs. Usually saddled on a horizontal limb in tall tree, rarely in a sapling. From 10 to 75 feet from the ground; if saddled on a limb, resembles a knot. Interior $1\frac{1}{2}$ inches deep and about the same in diameter. Resembles a large Hummingbird's nest.

   Southern New Jersey, southwestern Pennsylvania, southern Michigan, and Iowa south to Florida and the Gulf of Mexico.

   Blue-Gray Gnatcatcher

B. Over 2 Inches, Outside Diameter

1. Saucer-shaped, dainty, somewhat flat, compact, with fairly thick felted low sides and thin bottom; of fine grass, plant fibers, and bark shreds; lined with finer materials, sometimes with a little plant down, a few horsehairs, and bits of thread. Often the branch forms a portion of the bottom of the nest. Like that of the Hummingbird, it is frequently indistinguishable at a distance from a knot on the limb. Average size is $2\frac{3}{4}$ inches outside diameter by $1\frac{3}{4}$ inches deep, with inner cup $1\frac{3}{4}$ inches wide by $1\frac{1}{4}$ inches deep.

Northern Florida and Gulf of Mexico throughout eastern and central United States.

Wood Pewee

2. SEE I C c(1) d(1) 10   **Cerulean Warbler**

III. Felted Nests of Cottony Materials

A. In Forks of Bushes or Saplings

1. Cup-shaped, compact, well made, thick-walled; of silver-gray plant fibers, fine grasses, bark shreds, and plant down; lined with plant down, fine grasses, and sometimes long hair; usually placed in shrubs or low in trees of lawns and orchards near water. Often an especially deep nest will be found resulting from the building of a second floor to cover over and leave unhatched a Cowbird's egg deposited with the first set of warbler's eggs. In small willows or large shrubs, often near water.

   Eastern and central United States south to northern Georgia, southern Missouri, and Oklahoma. Also in mangroves in Florida Keys.

   Yellow Warbler

2. Cup-shaped, thin-walled, but firm and compact; of bark strips, leaf stalks, plant fibers, and plant down; lined with fine rootlets, grasses, hair, and sometimes a few feathers; usually built close to the trunk of the tree or bush, 3 to 30 feet or more high.

   Eastern and central United States south to North Carolina, northern Georgia, southern Alabama, Louisiana, and Oklahoma.

   American Redstart

83

3. Cup-shaped, compact, artistic; of fine grasses, bark strips, and moss; lined characteristically with thistledown.

> Eastern and central United States south to northern Georgia, northern Alabama, central Arkansas, and southern Oklahoma.

Common Goldfinch

B. On Horizontal Branch or in Upright Crotch of Small Tree

1. Of plant stems, weeds, thistledown, cotton, or wool, felted and lined with moss or cotton; sometimes built entirely of cotton. In small trees or bushes, 5 to 20 feet up.

> Texas, Oklahoma, Kansas, and southern Nebraska, occasionally east to western Louisiana and southwestern Missouri.

Scissor-tailed Flycatcher

2. Cup-shaped, thick-walled, neat, compact; of bark, plant fibers, spiders' webs, insect cocoons, and lined with plant fibers or feathers; usually decorated with bits of paper, bark, moss, and plant down or wool.

> Eastern and central United States south to Oklahoma, Missouri, Indiana, northern New Jersey, and, in mountains, to North Carolina.

Least Flycatcher

IV. Containing a Layer of Mud

A. Built in Trees

a(1). Under 4 inches, inside diameter

1. Cup-shaped, thick-walled, bulky, sometimes rough appearing; of coarse grasses, twigs, and rootlets, as well as paper, cloth, and string, with an inner wall of mud; lined usually with fine grass; commonly built in fruit or shade trees, but may be placed on projection of house or open shelf erected by man for the purpose. [See also IV B b(3) 1 and IX A a(2) 2]

    Eastern and central United States south to western South Carolina, northern Georgia, northern Louisiana, and northern Mississippi.

    Robin

2. Cup-shaped, compact, similar to nest of Robin but somewhat more hollowed; of leaves, rootlets, fine twigs, and weed stalks, with a foundation of leaves, an inner wall of mud or leaf mold, and a lining of fine rootlets; usually built in saplings.

    Southern South Dakota, central Minnesota, central Wisconsin, New York, and central New Hampshire south almost to Gulf of Mexico.

    Wood Thrush

3. Rather bulky, of layers of leaves, grass, and mud, often lined with fine grasses; in alders or

85

willows within a foot or two of water. In swampy woodlands.

Northern New York and northern New England.
Rusty Blackbird

4. Large and bulky, composed externally of a rough frame of twigs, stalks, bark, and rootlets, mixed and held together with a layer of mud; lined with fine rootlets, grasses, and horse and cow hairs; usually low, but sometimes 30 feet up, in trees or bushes; often in large colonies.

Western prairie country east to Minnesota, Wisconsin, northern Illinois, and Kansas.
Brewer's Blackbird

a(2). Over 4 inches, inside diameter
1. A large, bulky, rough structure of sticks, grass, bark strips, saw grass, seaweed, and roots, generally coated inside with mud. In small trees, bushes; in saplings; or in fully grown trees as high as 40 feet above ground; among reeds in swamps. [See also IV C 1]

Near salt water along coast from Delaware and Chesapeake Bay south to Florida Keys and west to Texas; also inland throughout Florida.
Boat-tailed Grackle

2. A loose, bulky structure of twigs, grass, weed stalks, frequently reinforced with mud, and lined with finer similar materials. Built preferably in a conifer, usually in or near a swamp, but often on farm lands; placed on a bough but often in a fork formed by topmost whorl of branches. Also sometimes built in a tree

cavity, in a hollow stub, or even in a bird house. [See also VIII A a(3) 28]

Southern New England, southern New York south between the Appalachians and the coast to Florida, and southern Louisiana.

Purple Grackle

3. Cup-shaped, coarse, bulky, similar to Robin's nest but larger. [See also IV B b(3) 2]

Canadian border south to Massachusetts and west of Appalachians (throughout Mississippi Valley and plains) to Louisiana and Texas.

Bronzed Grackle

B. Built on or in Buildings, on Bridges, or Against Rocks

b(1). Outer layer of mud with strengthening of grass or straw

1. Cup-shaped if built on a flat surface, cone-shaped if on a vertical surface, open at top; of mud mixed with grass and straw; lined with poultry feathers; usually built on a rafter inside barns or other buildings. [See also IX B b(1) 1]

Eastern and central United States south to North Carolina, northern Alabama, Tennessee, and Arkansas; also locally on Gulf Coast.

Barn Swallow

2. Gourd-shaped or shaped like a flask, retort, or bottle, with a narrow entrance on side leading into an enlarged chamber; of mud strengthened with straw and horsehair and scantily lined with a few dried grass stems and feathers;

built beneath eaves of buildings. [See also IX A a(3) 1]

Eastern and central United States south locally to western Virginia, northern Alabama, and Texas.
(Northern) Cliff (or Eaves) Swallow

b(2). Outer layer of mosses

1. Cup-shaped if built on a beam or rafter, semi-circular if attached to wall or side of overhanging rock; of mud, dry grass, and plant fibers; lined with finer fibers and hair and covered with moss. Average size: outer diameter, $4\frac{1}{2}$ inches; height, 4 inches; inner cup, $2\frac{1}{2}$ inches in diameter by $1\frac{3}{4}$ inches deep. [See also IX A a(4) 1]

Eastern and central United States south to northern Mississippi, Texas, and mountains of Georgia.
Eastern Phoebe

b(3). Outer layer of grasses

1. SEE IV A a(1) 1 and IX A a(2) 2   **Robin**

2. SEE IV A a(2) 3   **Bronzed Grackle**

C. Among Reeds in Swamps

1. SEE IV A a(2) 1   **Boat-tailed Grackle**

V. Made Chiefly of Bark, Fibers, Twigs, and Rootlets

A. Less than 2 Inches, Inside Diameter

a(1). Usually in conifers

1. Cup-shaped, somewhat variable in structure; of fine twigs, stiff dead grass, weeds, pine needles, spiders' webs, and cocoons; lined with fine black roots or hair, plant down, and stems of hair-cap moss (Polytrichum spp.); usually placed rather low on a limb away from trunk, but may be as high as 35 feet from the ground.

Minnesota, northern Wisconsin to northern Massachusetts, and, in Appalachians, to Virginia.

Magnolia Warbler

2. Cup-shaped; of twigs, grasses, moss, stems, with spiders' webbing interwoven with fine fabrics and knotted with numerous little balls, which are found upon the surface; lined with horse-hair. Exterior roughly made but more compact than that of the Magnolia Warbler, which it resembles; lining laid with precision and fashioned into a neat cup with the brim accurately turned into an almost perfect circle. Usually placed in low evergreens, near ground, in open fields.

Northern Maine and New Hampshire.

Cape May Warbler

3. Cup-shaped, rather bulky; of fine bark strips, stems, twigs, dried grass, weed stalks, bound with spiders' webs and lined with hair and feathers or plant down.

Northern Minnesota, northern Michigan, New Hampshire, Maine, and in mountains of New York and Massachusetts.

Myrtle Warbler

4. Cup-shaped, beautiful, compact, deep; of conifer twigs bound with caterpillars' or spiders' webs; lined with fine grasses, pine needles, bark strips, hair, or feathers; usually placed on horizontal or drooping limb; rarely low, commonly at height of 15 to 70 feet.

Eastern and central United States south to southern Minnesota, northern Ohio, New Jersey, Long Island, and, in mountains, to northern Georgia.

Black-throated Green Warbler

5. Cup-shaped, elegant, compact, but somewhat variable in size and materials; sometimes thick and heavily built, sometimes light and airy; commonly made of coniferous twigs, but sometimes including bark strips, pine needles, and lichens; lined with fine rootlets and hair, occasionally also fine grass and feathers; usually placed toward end of limb or near top of tree, at height up to 80 feet.

Canadian border south to central Minnesota, Wisconsin, central Michigan, southern New England, and, in Appalachians, to northern Georgia.

Blackburnian Warbler

6. Cup-shaped; of twiglets, strips of bark, and leaf stems, sometimes found with Spanish moss

or caterpillar silk or plant down; lined with soft vegetable down, hair, or feathers; compact and somewhat like a Pine Warbler's nest but without the black grapevine bark. In northern part of range usually placed in a sycamore, but in southern part of range usually placed on the horizontal branch of a pine but sometimes in a live oak, fastened to the limb by silky fibers; from 10 to 120 feet from the ground, usually concealed in Spanish moss or fine foliage.

Along Atlantic coastal plain from Florida north to Maryland and southern New Jersey (probably). Also Mississippi Valley from Gulf States north to southern Michigan and southern Wisconsin.

Yellow-throated Warbler

7. Cup-shaped; of twigs, mosses, grasses, rootlets, and lichens; lined with fine mosses or lichens and feathers; usually low in a spruce tree, rarely on the ground. In stunted spruces.

Northern Michigan, northern Maine, and mountains of New York, New Hampshire, Vermont, and Massachusetts.

Black-poll Warbler

8. Cup-shaped; of bark strips, weed stems, pine needles, and caterpillars' or spiders' webs; lined with pine needles, fern down, hair, bristles, or feathers; usually found in open pine woods on long limb at any distance from trunk and 10 to 50 feet high. In pine woods.

Eastern and central United States south to southern Florida and Gulf States.

Pine Warbler

9. Cup-shaped, frail, loosely constructed, rather shallow; of bark fibers, rootlets, weed stalks, and grasses; lined chiefly with hair.

North Dakota, central Minnesota, northern Illinois, and New England, south in mountains to Maryland.

(Eastern) Purple Finch

10. Saucer-shaped, rather flat, and somewhat large for size of bird; of grass or twigs, pine needles, rootlets, moss, lichens, and bark strips; lined with rootlets, plant down, fur, hair, feathers, or moss; usually well concealed among thick foliage, 8 to 30 feet from the ground.

Northern Minnesota, northern New England, and in mountains of North Carolina.

Pine Siskin

a(2). In bushes or saplings

1. Cup-shaped, neat, thick-walled, and rather bulky outside; of bark strips, rootlets, grasses, vines, twigs, and spiders' webs; neatly lined with fine black rootlets or horsehair; always decorated exteriorly with corky bits of wood and woolly parts of cocoons; bits of dead wood in bottom.

Northern fringe of eastern and central United States west to northern Minnesota and south to Massachusetts and, in mountains, to Georgia.

Black-throated Blue Warbler

2. Cup-shaped, rather loosely woven, not very neat; of bark strips, plant fibers, coarse grass, bunches of spiders' webs, and plant down; lined with rootlets, fine grasses, and horsehair;

usually in deciduous growth. In shrubby deciduous slashings and bushy pastures.

Eastern and central United States south to Nebraska, Illinois, northern Ohio, northern New Jersey, and, in uplands, to Tennessee and western
South Carolina.

Chestnut-sided Warbler

3. Cup-shaped; of soft strips of inner bark, plant
stems and other fibrous material, dry leaves,
spiders' webs, and cottony fibers; lined with
plant down, feathers, or golden-colored moss
stems; usually in a fork in the leafy top of a
low shrub in shrubby pastures or dry sprout-
land. In dry, bushy slashings and burns,
scrubby pine and oak barrens. In Florida mangroves are preferred.

Florida and Gulf States locally north to southern
New Hampshire, southern New York, southern
Ohio, southern Michigan, and eastern Nebraska.

Prairie Warbler

B. Over 2 Inches, Inside Diameter

b(1). Usually in conifers

1. Saucer-shaped, shallow; of twigs, rootlets, bark,
weed stalks, and usnea, lined with grass, moss,
and rootlets; usually set among a mass of fine
twigs projecting from the limb on which it
rests; 10 to 50 feet above the ground.

Northern Minnesota, northern Michigan, New
York, Massachusetts, and, in mountains, to North
Carolina.

Olive-sided Flycatcher

2. Compact, cup-shaped structure, little more
than 2 inches in diameter by 1 in depth; of

small twigs and moss smoothly and neatly lined with black, fibrous roots, moss, and hair; on a horizontal branch, toward end or near trunk; from 3 to 20 feet from the ground.

Northern Maine, the mountains of New Hampshire and Vermont, and the Adirondacks in New York.

Bay-breasted Warbler

b(2). In bushes or moderately low trees

1. Cup-shaped, rather bulky, somewhat ragged and loose exteriorly, but well cupped and brimmed; of dried weed stems, grasses, small twigs, and mosses, and often containing bits of cloth, feathers, wool, and pieces of string; lined with fine dry grass, plant down, rootlets, and hair; generally placed at the extremity of a branch, often in a bush or low tree on a river bank; also found in such peculiar locations as on a stump, a fence post, in an eaves trough, or on a fence rail. Average size: outside, $3\frac{1}{4}$ inches by $5\frac{1}{2}$ inches; inside, diameter 3 inches, depth $1\frac{3}{4}$ inches. In rural country.

Eastern and central United States south to Gulf of Mexico.

Eastern Kingbird

2. Cup-shaped; of twigs, leaves, weed bark, wool, cocoons, hair, string, down, rags, and paper; in trees and bushes from 5 to 50 feet up, but usually low; also in fence posts, corners of houses, or any other convenient spot. [See also IX A a(5) 1]

Eastern limit is western Minnesota, western Iowa, Kansas, and Oklahoma.

Arkansas Kingbird

3. Cup-shaped, bulky, rather deep; rough externally; of bark strips, plant down, plant fibers,
leaves, rootlets, rags, paper, and twine; lined
with finer bits of these materials and sometimes
with horsehair or wool; usually placed on
nearly horizontal branch of tree, 4 to 40 feet
from ground, though sometimes built in bush.

Eastern and central United States south to North
Carolina, northern Georgia, and Kansas.

Cedar Waxwing

4. Large, carelessly constructed affair; of twigs,
rootlets, weed stems, coarse grass, corn stalks,
paper, and wool, and thickly lined with feathers, hair, and wool. Located on thorny trees
(hawthorns), in hedges or thickets, usually
within 10 feet of the ground.

Eastern and central United States locally to
Florida and Gulf Coast.

Loggerhead Shrike

5. Cup-shaped, rather large and somewhat flat,
and so thin that the eggs may usually be seen
from below; of fine bark strips, weed stems,
grasses, and twigs; lined with fine rootlets;
usually placed near end of horizontal tree
branch, 10 to 30 feet above the ground. In
woodlands and groves (preferably oak).

Eastern and central United States south to western South Carolina, northern Georgia, northern
Alabama, and Kansas.

Scarlet Tanager

6. Cup-shaped; of bark strips, rootlets, a few
leaves, and grass. A firm structure but so thin
and shallow that the eggs may be seen from

beneath; in Southern States sometimes more compactly built by the addition of moss and down. Usually near end of horizontal limb of deciduous tree, from 5 to 30 feet from the ground. Generally found in woods but sometimes in villages and thickly settled towns.

Florida and Gulf of Mexico north to Delaware, central Ohio, southern Wisconsin, southern Iowa, and southeastern Nebraska.

Summer Tanager

7. A carelessly constructed, loosely put-together nest of small twigs, strips of bark, weed stems, grasses, and rootlets, lined with fine grass or hair; from 3 to 30 feet from the ground in tree, vine, or bush, but usually quite low; sometimes on top of bush-covered fence or vine-covered stump, or in brush heap.

Eastern and central United States east of plains and north to southern New York, Lake Erie, southern Minnesota, and southeastern South Dakota.

Cardinal

8. Saucer-shaped, loosely made, and insecurely placed in a fork; of vegetable fibers, grass, and twigs; lined with finer materials, rootlets, or pine needles; in high bushes or trees, 5 to 20 feet above the ground.

Eastern and central United States south to Kansas, southern Missouri, central Ohio, central New Jersey, and, in mountains, to northern Georgia.

Rose-breasted Grosbeak

9. Saucer-shaped; of small twigs, grass, rootlets, bark strips; lined with fine rootlets or horse-

hair; usually in top of conifer from 15 to 20 feet up, but sometimes in other trees.

Northern Michigan. Recently found nesting in New England.

(Eastern) Evening Grosbeak

VI. Made Chiefly of Grasses, Rootlets, Leaves, and Straw

A. In Bushes, Weeds, or Ferns

a(1). Under 2 inches, inside diameter

1. Cup-shaped; of grasses, weeds, and a few leaves; lined with fine grass and sometimes with hair or feathers. Open, bushy places.

   > Eastern and central United States south to central parts of Gulf States, and northwestern Florida.
   > **Indigo Bunting**

2. A compact, cup-shaped structure of leaves, grass, rootlets, bark strips, twigs, and lined with fine grasses and horsehair (sometimes). Resembles nest of Indigo Bunting but more neatly made. Built in bushes, saplings, and tall trees. [See also VI B b(1) 5]

   > Gulf States north to southeastern North Carolina, northern Mississippi, central Arkansas, and southern Kansas.
   > **(Eastern) Painted Bunting**

3. SEE VI B b(1) 6 and Nests On or In the Ground I A a(1) 3   **Dickcissel**

4. Cup-shaped, delicate, cleverly interwoven; of fine grass and rootlets and lined with hair of horse, cow, or deer; sometimes constructed entirely of horsehair; usually found in a bush or

vine, but at times also built in a tree, such as apple or red cedar. [See also VI B b(1) 8]

Eastern and central United States south to northern parts of Gulf States.

(Eastern) Chipping Sparrow

5. SEE Nests On or In the Ground I A a(4) 2
Clay-colored Sparrow

6. SEE Nests On or In the Ground I A a(4) 3 and II A a(1) 15   **(Eastern) Field Sparrow**

a(2). Over 2 inches, inside diameter
1. SEE Nests On or In the Ground III A a(4) 4
Limpkin

2. Cup-shaped; of leaves, mosses, grass, stems, and twigs; lined with rootlets; usually built in spruce or fir trees. [See also VI B b(1) 1]

Northern Michigan, northern New York, northern New England, and, in mountains, to West Virginia.

Olive-backed Thrush

3. Cup-shaped; of coarse grasses, moss, rootlets, and leaves; lined with grasses and rootlets; nest usually built in spruce and fir scrub on mountain tops. [See also VI B b(1) 2]

Northern New England and New York south to Catskills and higher Berkshires in Massachusetts.

Gray-cheeked Thrush

4. SEE VIII A a(3) 23 and Nests On or In the Ground II A(1) 6   **Veery**

5. Cup-shaped, rather large, compact; of grasses, leaves, and bark strips, well interwoven and lined with fine grasses; often well concealed in tangle of grapevine, smilax, and briers, 1 to 5 feet above ground. In brier thickets and bushy clearings.

> Massachusetts (local), central New York, Michigan, and southern Minnesota south to northern Florida and Gulf of Mexico.

Yellow-breasted Chat

6. See VI B b(1) 7 and Nests On or In the Ground I A a(5) 11　　**(Eastern) Lark Sparrow**

7. See VI B b(1) 9 and Nests On or In the Ground I A a(1) 7 and II A a(2) 8　　**Song Sparrow**

B. In Trees

b(1). Cup-shaped

1. See VI A a(2) 2　　**Olive-backed Thrush**

2. See VI A a(2) 3　　**Gray-cheeked Thrush**

3. Of fine vegetable fiber, grass, leaves, and moss; lined with hair; in conifers close to ground.

> Along northern fringe of eastern and central United States west to northern Minnesota.

Tennessee Warbler

4. A compact, well built structure of dried grass, plant fibers, leaves, rootlets; lined with fine brown rootlets and sometimes with horsehair; usually a cast snakeskin is incorporated into the nest. Usually placed on the low branch of a

tree but sometimes found in low brambles along roadsides and on the borders of woods.

Gulf States north to Maryland, southern Illinois, and Nebraska.

(Eastern) Blue Grosbeak

5. SEE VI A a(1) 2   **(Eastern) Painted Bunting**

6. SEE VI A a(1) 3 and Nests On or In the Ground
   I A a(1) 3   **Dickcissel**

7. SEE VI A a(2) 6 and Nests On or In the Ground
   I A a(5) 11   **(Eastern) Lark Sparrow**

8. SEE VI A a(1) 4   **(Eastern) Chipping Sparrow**

9. SEE VI A a(2) 7 and Nests On or In the Ground
   I A a(1) 7 and II A a(2) 8   **Song Sparrow**

b(2). Spherical
   1. Bulky, domed, loosely constructed, with entrance on side; of grass and straw; warmly lined with feathers; also built in birdhouses, electric-light hoods, cornices, waterspouts, and similar places about buildings. [See also VIII A a(3) 27 and IX A a(5) 2]

   Throughout eastern and central United States.

   House Sparrow

VII. Containing Twigs or Sticks

A. Very Large, 30 to 60 Inches, Outside Diameter

1. A simple platform of sticks, usually in low bushes, 5 to 10 feet above ground, but also in high trees.

> Extreme southern Florida and the Florida Keys.
> **Great White Heron**

2. Of sticks $\frac{1}{4}$ to $\frac{1}{2}$ inch in diameter; lined with finer twigs and grass; 3 feet or more across; usually built high in trees and near extremity of branches, but sometimes in bushes or even on the ground, and usually in wooded swamps. A colony nester; several nests may be built in the same tree.

> Florida Keys and Gulf Coast north throughout eastern and central United States.
> **Great Blue Heron**

3. SEE Nests On or In the Ground VI B 2
> **Golden Eagle**

4. Usually in or near top of high tree; of sticks and rubbish; flat-topped, with egg cavity 4 to 5 inches deep and 20 inches across; lined with grass or pine needles. May be repaired and used year after year until it is from 5 to 8

feet across and 8 feet or more high. Chiefly near ocean, rivers, and lakes.

Gulf of Mexico north throughout eastern and central United States.

Bald Eagle

5. Cup-shaped; of sticks, twigs, driftwood, and stalks of weeds; often lined with grass or seaweed and a few feathers; sometimes containing such materials as old shoes, bones, and pieces of dry cow dung; built near water, usually in a treetop, but sometimes on buildings, telephone poles, or chimneys. Frequently old nests are repaired, for the Osprey is accustomed to utilize the same nesting site year after year, and as a result of building on the old nest and repairing it the nest in time becomes almost as large as that of an eagle. Near water. [See also IX A a(6) 1]

Gulf of Mexico north throughout eastern and central United States.

Osprey

6. A large bulky platform of branches, with a slight depression, and lined with small sticks, roots, and grasses, frequently without a lining. In trees and bushes, sometimes in cliffs (Texas).

Central peninsular Florida and southern Texas.
Audubon's Caracara

7. Cup-shaped; of large sticks, well interlaced, lined with coarse grass, bark strips, hair, wool, and, in maritime sites, with seaweed. Near top of thick-topped coniferous tree or on shelf of

high cliff, usually well sheltered by projecting rock above. [See also Nests On or In the Ground VI B 5]

Maine, Michigan, Minnesota, and locally in Appalachians to Georgia; occasional along coast from New Jersey to North Carolina.

Raven

B. Smaller, 15 to 30 Inches, Outside Diameter

b(1). Saucer-shaped or flattened

1. Very bulky; of sticks; lined with hemlock or pine twigs, sometimes a little grass or weed stalks, birch or coniferous bark; near the trunk or well out in fork of a large limb.

   Northern Michigan, northern New York, and northern New England, and sparingly in mountains to Pennsylvania.

   (Eastern) Goshawk

2. Of small sticks; lined chiefly with twigs, sometimes with bark, rarely with grass, moss, or leaves; built on branches against the trunk of white pine, preferably, but also in other coniferous trees.

   Northern Florida and Gulf Coast north throughout eastern and central United States.

   Sharp-shinned Hawk

3. Clean, substantial structure, rather broad and flat in white pines but not so broad in deciduous trees; of dried sticks; lined with chips of outer bark of pine or oak; if placed in a pine tree, against the trunk at the base of

several branches; if in an oak, in the fork of a branch.

Eastern and central United States south to Gulf of Mexico.

Cooper's Hawk

4. Quite flat and shallow; of large twigs or sticks; lined with strips of inner bark, grasses, weeds, dead leaves, corn husks, or moss, and a few sprigs of pine, cedar, or hemlock; built higher than a Red-shoulder's, often nearly at top of tall trees, preferably oak or white pine. In dry woodland.

Eastern and central United States south to Gulf of Mexico and northern Florida.

Red-tailed Hawk

5. Well built, substantial, rather flat on top, somewhat smaller than a Red-tail's; of sticks and twigs, well decorated with bits of white down and mixed with strips of inner bark, dry leaves, and lichens; inner cavity lined with finer shreds of inner bark, soft mosses, or lichens, and sprigs of pine, cedar, or hemlock; often decorated with leaves of deciduous trees when they become available; usually on branches next to the trunk or in crotch of tree, preferably in pine or oak. In moist woodlands and river timber.

Eastern and central United States south to Florida and Gulf of Mexico and west to Great Plains.

Red-shouldered Hawk

6. Sometimes crudely built, at other times well built with handsome, well hollowed and lined

interior and encircling fringe; of twigs, sticks, and sometimes mosses; lined with chips of outer bark of oak or pine, sometimes with sprigs of pine and oak leaves; usually built in a tree but sometimes on a branching stub. In dry forests of wooded hills.

Gulf of Mexico north throughout eastern and central United States.

Broad-winged Hawk

7. Of small branches and twigs, and lined with a few leaves, moss, or feathers; generally placed in the tallest trees toward the end of horizontal branches; but sometimes placed in bushes, in hedges, or on rocky ledge of cliff. (See also Nests On or In the Ground VI B 1); sometimes old nests are rehabilitated.

Plains of Minnesota, Nebraska, Kansas.

Swainson's Hawk

8. Of cypress twigs and moss; in tall trees in forested swamps.

Rare and local in southern Florida and the Keys.

Short-tailed Hawk

9. Of sticks, lined with grasses, leaves, moss, and feathers. Near top of tall tree in coniferous forests. Sometimes on ledges and occasionally in a hollow tree. [See also VIII A a(3) 6 and Nests On or In the Ground VI B 4]

Northern fringe of eastern and central United States.

(Eastern) Pigeon Hawk

b(2). Cup-shaped

1. Of sticks, lined with a little moss. In top of tall tree, near watercourses.

    Found chiefly in river swamps of Florida, South Carolina, and Louisiana.

    Swallow-tailed Kite

2. Of sticks and twigs; lined with bark or with down from the mother's breast; rarely builds own nest, preferring to use the deserted nest of a Red-tailed or Red-shouldered Hawk or Crow; containing, as a rule, bones, fur, and feathers, and other refuse of food. Sometimes impregnated with the odor of skunk.

    Eastern and central United States south to Florida and Texas.

    Great Horned Owl

3. Of sticks and twigs; lined with bark; usually in a conifer; commonly uses the deserted nest of a bird such as a Crow, Heron, or Hawk.

    Eastern and central United States south to Virginia and northern Texas.

    Long-eared Owl

4. Large, bulky; of strong sticks; lined with strips of grapevine bark, grasses, moss, and fine roots. Sometimes the interior has a warm yellowish-brown color. Occasionally the nest will contain such materials as seaweed, corn stalks, pieces of rope and twine, feathers, dried cow and horse manure. In trees, averaging about 30 feet from the ground.

    Eastern and central United States south to Florida and Texas.

    Crow

b(3). Like platform

1. SEE Nests On or In the Ground IV A 1
   ### (Eastern) Brown Pelican

2. SEE Nests On or In the Ground VI A 1
   ### Double-crested Cormorant

3. Chiefly of sticks, with leaves, dry grass, roots, and moss; lined with moss and rootlets. In small trees or bushes, but sometimes attached to the upper branches of a high tree and always over water.

   Gulf Coast and Florida north locally to North Carolina, northeastern Tennessee, southern Illinois, and Arkansas.

   ### Water-Turkey

4. Of sticks; usually in a tall tree but sometimes on bush or other growth; in communities in marshes and in wooded swamps.

   Gulf Coast and Florida north to Tennessee and New Jersey.

   ### American Egret

5. Of sticks and twigs, usually in low trees or bushes in a swamp; in southern mangrove swamps.

   Along coast from North Carolina to Louisiana and Texas; north rarely to New Jersey.

   ### Snowy Egret

6. Of sticks and twigs; lined with smaller twigs, rootlets, straw, and grasses; well built for a heron; in low bushes or on the ground.

   Gulf Coast of Texas; rare in southern Florida (becoming increasingly resident in the Keys).

   ### Reddish Egret

7. A frail platform of sticks; in mangrove or willow swamps; in colonies or in company with other herons.

   Coastal North Carolina to Texas.
   Louisiana Heron

8. Frail, loose platform of sticks and twigs, slightly hollowed, with finer twigs for lining; usually over water and 3 to 10 feet high in bushes or small trees. Nesting in colonies of this and other species.

   Gulf Coast and Florida north to New Jersey and Massachusetts (casually).
   Little Blue Heron

9. Frail, loosely put together; of small sticks; 10 to 12 inches in diameter; usually in a low tree or bush near water. Unlike nests of many other herons, it is commonly built alone rather than in a colony.

   Gulf of Mexico north throughout eastern and central United States.
   (Eastern) Green Heron

10. Vary greatly in size and construction, from small, crudely built platforms of sticks, lined with twigs, to large, well built structures of sticks, lined with twigs, roots, grass, and pine needles; in from very low to quite high trees, toward the tips of the branches; in a wooded swamp, but sometimes in dry hillside thicket. A colony nester.

    Florida and Gulf of Mexico north throughout eastern and central United States.
    Black-crowned Night Heron

11. Substantially built; of good-sized sticks; perhaps well hollowed and lined with twigs, fibrous roots, or weeds; from 2 to 25 feet or more above the water. A colony nester, often nesting with other species. Size of nest: 18 to 20 inches, outside diameter. Chiefly swamps.

> Gulf of Mexico north to Missouri, Tennessee, Maryland, New Jersey, and casually Long Island and Massachusetts.
>
> **Yellow-crowned Night Heron**

12. Of sticks; in trees, sometimes very high, as much as 100 feet above the ground. The same sites are occupied each year and the nests become very bulky from the addition of material each season. In colonies in swampy regions.

> Chiefly near coast, from South Carolina to Texas.
>
> **Wood Ibis**

13. SEE I B 1   **White Ibis**

14. A platform of sticks in dense tropical marshes, usually in cypress trees or mangrove bushes, from 8 to 20 feet above ground.

> Locally in southern Florida, on Texas coast, and locally in Louisiana.
>
> **Roseate Spoonbill**

15. Of sticks, leaves, and grasses; in low bushes.

> Dry Tortugas, Florida.
>
> **Noddy**

16. A platform of sticks with sides of bark, twigs, and grasses, lined with grapevine or other bark, grass, and a few leaves, usually with some pine

needles; commonly in pine or other conifer in coastal regions or near some body of water; from 15 to 50 feet up, sometimes higher and frequently near top.

Southern New England south to Florida and along coast to eastern Texas; also in Florida and in river valleys such as Hudson and Delaware.

Fish Crow

C. Small, Under 15 Inches, Outside Diameter

c(1). Usually in evergreens

1. Bulky, high-walled, neatly built structure of twigs, bark strips, grasses, with warm soft lining of lichens or mosses and feathers or down, the whole being fastened together by small bunches of spiders' nests and cocoons. Usually placed on horizontal branches against the trunk or in an upright crotch. From 6 to 8 feet above the ground.

Northern fringe of eastern and central United States.

Canada Jay

2. Cup-shaped, bulky, carelessly built, usually with a ragged rim; of sticks, twigs, and rootlets interwoven; lined with bark strips, feathers, leaves, or grass; sometimes containing a wide assortment of materials, such as rags, paper, string, pine needles, in fact anything that may capture the bird's fancy; in a crotch 10 to 20 feet above the ground.

Eastern and central United States south to Florida and Gulf of Mexico.

Blue Jay

3. Of twigs and rootlets, with a well woven inner nest of finer twigs, grasses, and bark strips; usually in conifers.

Mountains of northern New England.
(Canadian) Pine Grosbeak

4. Loosely constructed; of evergreen twigs, shreds of bark, and rootlets; lined with moss, leaves, grass, hair, or fur well felted together, and generally some bits of hemlock or cedar tips. Usually built rather low, within 20 feet of the ground, in thick foliage of a conifer, but sometimes quite high and in a bare deciduous tree.

Nests locally in Appalachians from New England to Tennessee.
Red Crossbill

5. Twigs and strips of birch bark, covered exteriorly with usnea; lined with soft moss and hair; in fork of an evergreen in deep forests.

Northern edge of eastern and central United States.
White-winged Crossbill

c(2). In chimney, inside barn wall or similar structure, and at times in primitive site—a hollow tree

1. Semicircular basket or hammock of twigs, glued together and to the chimney or similar structure with the glutinous saliva of the Swift; if in chimney, generally about 10 feet from the top. [See also IX B b(2) 1]

Eastern and central United States south to Gulf of Mexico.
Chimney Swift

c(3). Inside the loose bark of trees

1. Cup-shaped; of slim twigs, bark strips, moss, dead wood; lined sometimes with a few spiders' cocoons, feathers, and hair; placed rather low; occasionally found in a knothole or a deserted nest of woodpecker. [See also VIII A a(3) 17]

> Canadian border south to eastern Nebraska, northern Indiana, New York, Massachusetts, and, in mountains, to North Carolina.
>
> **Brown Creeper**

c(4). In trees or bushes, vines or tangles

1. Of sticks, lined with leaves or Spanish moss. In trees 12 to 50 feet above ground, generally in a high treetop. Sometimes old nest of some other species is used and remodeled.

> Gulf States north to Kansas, southern Missouri, and southwestern Tennessee; also east to north-eastern Florida and South Carolina.
>
> **Mississippi Kite**

2. A rather flat, carelessly put-together structure of sticks and twigs, grasses, and old leaves, and lined with a few dried heads of saw grass; about 1 foot in diameter, with a cavity 3 inches deep; in a bush, small tree, or clump of grass.

> Locally in fresh-water marshes of Florida.
>
> **Everglade Kite**

3. A crude platform of sticks, with little or no lining of grasses; on the whole, a bulky structure for a pigeon. In low trees and bushes. In colonies.

> Southern tip of Florida and Florida Keys.
>
> **White-crowned Pigeon**

4. Hollowed platform, frail and so loosely constructed that the eggs appear to be in danger
of falling through the interstices; of sticks and
small twigs with a few straws and weed stalks
and sometimes leaves or a little moss; often
placed in the lower branches of a pine.

> Eastern and central United States (except north-
> ern Maine) south to Gulf Coast.
>
> **Mourning Dove**

5. A frail structure of twigs, sometimes with the
addition of pine needles. Usually from 2 to 6
feet above the ground in stumps, vines, bushes,
and small trees, but often on the ground in
fields or weed patches. [See also Nests On or In
the Ground I A a(2) 1]

> Coastal Plain and low country from South Caro-
> lina to Texas. Occasional in North Carolina.
>
> **(Eastern) Ground Dove**

6. A loosely made structure of a few dry sticks; in
low branches of trees and in bushes. Mangrove
swamps.

> Southwestern coast of Florida and Keys.
>
> **Mangrove Cuckoo**

7. Shallow platform, frail, rather ragged; of small
twigs rarely over 4 or 5 inches long, rootlets,
and bark strips; lined with catkins, dry blossoms of horse chestnut and other flowering
plants, tufts of grass, pine needles, and mosses;
usually in low tree or thicket.

> Eastern and central United States south to Flor-
> ida Keys and Gulf of Mexico.
>
> **Yellow-billed Cuckoo**

8. Platform, similar to that of the Yellow-billed but more firmly constructed; of sticks and twigs; lined with catkins, dried leaves, and similar materials.

   Eastern and central United States south to Arkansas and North Carolina and, in mountains, to Georgia.

   Black-billed Cuckoo

9. A frail, loosely built structure of twigs, lined with small plant stems and moss; in tree or bush, usually in low mangroves or live oaks but sometimes high in trees; in or near woodland.

   Locally along east and west coasts of Florida and rarely to South Carolina. Most common in Florida Keys.

   Gray Kingbird

10. A flat, compact structure of small dry sticks, leaves, and plant stems, lined with moss, fibrous plant stems, and often with wool and feathers; in low scrub.

    Local in scrub regions of Florida Peninsula.

    Florida Jay

11. Cup-shaped, bulky; of twigs, leaves, moss, bark strips, weeds, grass, rags, cotton string, rootlets, feathers, hair, down, and tree blossoms; lined with fine rootlets, horsehair, dried grass; on branch, in fork among twigs; occasionally placed in fence corners, or in hollow top of post or stump or decayed tree trunk. Usually from 3 to 20 feet above the ground, in tree,

shrub, vine, or dense tangle. [See also VIII A a(3) 22]

> Massachusetts, Ohio, Illinois, southern Iowa, Nebraska south to the Gulf of Mexico.

(Eastern) Mockingbird

12. Cup-shaped; rather rough, straggly, and bulky outwardly, but inwardly neatly lined; of twigs, grasses, leaves, and pieces of paper, lined with rootlets and strips of grapevine bark; usually placed in dense thickets, bushes, or low trees, 3 to 10 feet from the ground.

> Eastern and central United States south to northern Florida, Louisiana, and southeastern Texas.

Catbird

13. Cup-shaped, bulky, loosely built; of sticks, twigs, leaves, bark strips, and weed stalks; lined with rootlets; inside diameter over 3 inches; placed not very far from the ground in brush pile, bush, vine, or low tree. In thickets and shrubbery.

> Eastern and central United States south to central Florida and Gulf of Mexico.

(Eastern) Brown Thrasher

VIII. In Holes in Trees or Stumps, in Birdhouses or Similar Places

A. Nesting Singly

a(1). Drilling nesting cavity but building no nest in bottom; using chips of wood only

   1. Opening with diameter of $2\frac{1}{2}$ inches, cavity from 10 to 20 inches deep, 6 inches across the bottom. In various trees, dead or alive. Often uses natural cavities and sometimes strange places—as barns and icehouses, drilling through wall to haymow or insulating material. [See also IX A a(5) 3]

      Eastern and central United States south to Florida and Gulf of Mexico.

                            Flicker

   2. Opening somewhat triangular in shape, broader at base, angular at top, about $3\frac{1}{2}$ inches across. Cavity 15 to 26 inches deep, 7 to 8 inches across at top, 6 inches or more at bottom. In deep woods or edge of heavy woodland. Usually in dead, sound, but sometimes live deciduous trees.

      Eastern and central United States south to Florida and Gulf of Mexico.

                Pileated Woodpecker

   3. Opening about $1\frac{3}{4}$ inches in diameter; about 12 inches deep. In tree, stump, post, or pole,

from 16 to 50 feet from the ground. Usually nests in forests but also on open land.

Florida and Gulf of Mexico north to Delaware, Lake Erie, southeastern Minnesota, and southeastern South Dakota.

Red-bellied Woodpecker

4. Opening slightly elliptical, about 1¾ by 2 inches in diameter. Cavity 8 to 24 inches deep, gourd-shaped, about 3½ by 4½ inches across at the bottom; in telephone pole, dead treetop, stub, or stump, from 5 to 80 feet above the ground. Sometimes in natural cavity. [See also VIII A a(3) 7]

Gulf of Mexico north to southern New England, western New York, southern Michigan, and Minnesota.

Red-headed Woodpecker

5. Opening about 1½ inches in diameter, circular; cavity averaging 14 inches deep; gourd-shaped; 5 inches diameter at widest point. In large dead trees, usually birches, often near water.

Eastern and central United States south to western Massachusetts, northern Ohio, Indiana, Missouri, and, in mountains, to North Carolina.

Yellow-bellied Sapsucker

6. Opening slightly elliptical, 1⅞ inches high and 1½ inches wide; cavity gourd-shaped, 10 to 12 inches or more deep, 4½ inches wide at bottom. Usually in living trees in dry upland deciduous woodland, though sometimes in maple swamps or apple orchards.

Gulf of Mexico north throughout eastern and central United States.

Hairy Woodpecker

7. Opening about 1¼ inches in diameter, circular; cavity gourd-shaped, 8 to 12 inches deep. Generally in dead or dying wood.

> Gulf of Mexico north throughout eastern and central United States.

Downy Woodpecker

8. Usually in a living pine but sometimes in a deciduous tree, from 25 to 50 feet above the ground; depth of cavity 8 inches to a foot; gourd-shaped; there is generally a glazed patch of gum around the nesting hole. Pine woodlands.

> Gulf States north to southeastern Virginia, western Kentucky, and southern Missouri.

Red-cockaded Woodpecker

9. Opening about 1¾ inches to 2 inches in diameter expanding to gourd shape and from 9 to 18 inches deep. Opening beveled on lower edge. Either in living or dead tree of coniferous forests.

> Occasional in northern parts of eastern and central United States.

Arctic Three-toed Woodpecker

10. Opening about 1½ inches in diameter; about 10 or 12 inches deep. Opening beveled on lower edge, cavity gourd-shaped; in spruce, larch, balsam, or cedar tree, usually in tree killed by insects, fire, or water.

> Occasional in northern parts of eastern and central United States.

American Three-toed Woodpecker

a(2). Using hole excavated by woodpecker, natural cavity, or bird box; adding little or no nesting

material, placing eggs on chips left by woodpecker or litter left by some previous occupant,
as mouse or squirrel

1. Florida and Gulf of Mexico north throughout
   eastern and central United States.

   Sparrow Hawk

2. Massachusetts (occasional), Ohio, southern
   Wisconsin, and Nebraska south to Florida and
   Gulf of Mexico.

   Barn Owl

   NOTE: The Barn Owl frequently makes use of old
   buildings or church steeples, where it
   scrapes a nest in rubbish on a shelf. [See
   also IX A a(2) 3]

3. Eastern and central United States south to
   Florida and Texas.   **Screech Owl**

4. Eastern and central United States south to
   Florida and Texas.   **Barred Owl**

   NOTE: The Barred Owl may rebuild and reline
   for use the old nest of a Red-shouldered or
   Cooper's Hawk or of a squirrel.

5. Eastern and central United States south to
   northern Indiana, northern Illinois, and mountains of Pennsylvania, Maryland, and West
   Virginia.

   Saw-whet Owl

a(3). Using woodpecker hole, natural cavity (or
   sometimes excavating cavity), or bird box and
   building nest at bottom of cavity

   1. Nest of down from breast of female on punky
      wood of hole, sometimes on leaves which squir-

rel may previously have carried into cavity. Down grayish-white or pale mouse-gray with nearly pure white centers. In wooded swamps and river timber, apple orchards, or shade trees about farm buildings.

Gulf of Mexico north throughout eastern and central United States.

Wood Duck

2. Nest of grass, leaves, and moss and lined with light-gray down, each feather with a paler center. Nest may be in a hole from 6 to 8 to 50 or 60 feet above the ground, usually over or near water. It may be on level with and scarcely back from hole or at the bottom of hollow 6, 10, 15 feet or even more below entrance, which may vary from 15 inches to diameter so small as scarcely to admit bird. In forested country, generally about lakes or rivers.

Along northern edge of eastern and central United States.

American Goldeneye

3. Nest of grasses and weeds and lined with down from breast of female. In forests near water and often high above ground or water; sometimes in wooded swamps.

Eastern and central United States south locally or rarely to Southern States.

Hooded Merganser

4. Nest of grasses, twigs, leaves, and lichens, lined with grayish-white down; usually in hollow tree or in top of broken stub about woodlands

and rivers; sometimes on the ground. [See also Nests On or In the Ground II A a(1) 1]

Along northern edge of eastern and central United States.

American Merganser

5. SEE Nests On or In the Ground II A a(5) 1
Turkey Vulture

6. SEE VII B b(1) 9 and Nests On or In the Ground VI B 4   **(Eastern) Pigeon Hawk**

7. SEE VIII A a(1) 4   **Red-headed Woodpecker**

8. Nest bulky, filling bottom of cavity; of grass, leaves, small twigs, moss, rootlets, bark, hair, and pine needles; lined with finer materials. Often containing a cast snakeskin, strip of cellophane or onionskin. Inner cup from $2\frac{3}{4}$ to $3\frac{1}{2}$ inches in diameter and $1\frac{1}{2}$ to 2 inches deep.

Eastern and central United States south to Florida and Gulf Coast.

Crested Flycatcher

9. Nest open, cup-shaped; of grasses and straw, profusely lined with (preferably) white feathers and sometimes pine needles. In open wooded swamps or about farm lands.

Eastern and central United States south to Virginia, northeastern Arkansas, and Kansas.

Tree Swallow

10. Nest of plant fibers, leaves, and moss; lined with hair, plant down, wool, or feathers. Often

excavates nesting hole in decaying stump or stub.

New Jersey, Ohio, Missouri, and Oklahoma south
Eastern and central United States south to Kansas, Missouri, Illinois, Ohio, Pennsylvania, northern New Jersey, and, in mountains, to North Carolina.

Black-capped Chickadee

11. Nest of fine dry grasses, shreds of fibrous bark, with a warm lining of feathers, cattle hair, and fur of smaller animals.

New Jersey, Ohio, Missouri, and Oklahoma south to Florida and Gulf of Mexico.

Carolina Chickadee

12. Nest of moss and lichens or fern down and fur felted together, sometimes lined with feathers and fur; usually rather low. Often excavates nesting hole in decaying stub or tree. Spruce forests.

Mountains of northern edge of eastern and central United States.

Brown-capped Chickadee

13. Nest of moss, leaves, grass, bark, hair, feathers; from 4 to 65 feet from the ground, usually rather low.

Florida and Gulf of Mexico north to northern New Jersey, Lake Erie, Illinois, Iowa, and Nebraska.

Tufted Titmouse

14. Nest of bark shreds, fine grasses, leaves, hair, and feathers. May excavate hole in decaying

stump or stub, as Chickadee. In woodlands and orchards.

Eastern and central United States south to central Florida and Gulf Coast.

White-breasted Nuthatch

15. Nest may be of bark shreds, lined with feathers; sometimes of no material except the chips of the excavation; usually in conifers, in which case pitch is usually smeared on the bark about the entrance hole. May be excavated by the bird in decaying stub, with entrance 1 inch in diameter.

Northern Minnesota, Michigan, northern New England, and, in Appalachians, to North Carolina.

Red-breasted Nuthatch

16. Nest of small bits of grass, cotton, fine parts of pine needles, wool, and feathers. In a hole in a dead stump or tree, from 1 to 40 feet up; depth of cavity from 8 to 12 inches.

Florida and Gulf of Mexico north to coastal Delaware and southern Missouri.

Brown-headed Nuthatch

17. SEE VII C c(3) 1   **Brown Creeper**

18. Nest bulky; of small sticks, twigs, and grass, lined with strips of bark, hair, or feathers; generally filling the hole, bird box, or crevice in which it is built. May be located anywhere, in outbuildings, boxes, stumps, old tin cans, watering pots, or any other hollow object. [See also IX A a(3) 2 and IX A a(5) 4]

Eastern and central United States south to Virginia, Kentucky, southern Missouri, and central-western Texas.

House Wren

19. SEE Nests On or In the Ground II B b(1) 1
Winter Wren

20. Nest of leaves, twigs, chips, dried grasses, hay, rootlets, and spiders' webs; warmly lined with soft materials, such as fur, hair, and feathers. May be located anywhere in outbuildings, boxes, stumps, old tin cans, watering pots, or any other hollow object.

Mississippi Valley and southern Appalachian Plateau from central Pennsylvania, southern Michigan, northern Illinois, and southern Nebraska south to central Georgia, Alabama, Mississippi, and Arkansas.

Bewick's Wren

21. SEE IX A a(2) 1 and Nests On or In the Ground II A a(1) 5 and II B b(1) 2

Carolina Wren

22. SEE VII C c(4) 11   **Mockingbird**

23. SEE VI A a(2) 4 and Nests On or In the Ground II A a(1) 6   **Veery**

24. Nest usually of fine grasses, but may contain a few leaves, rootlets, fine twigs, hair, and feathers.

Eastern and central United States south to Florida and Gulf of Mexico.

Eastern Bluebird

25. Nest bulky and untidy; of grass or straw, sometimes with twigs, seaweed, corn husks; lined sparingly with feathers or moss.

> Eastern and central United States south to Gulf of Mexico.

Starling

26. Nest of moss, grass, leaves, lichens, bark strips, rootlets, bits of decaying wood, and other vegetable substances and carefully lined with moss, rarely with hair and feathers; from 2 to 15 feet up and almost always in a stump standing or leaning over water; usually in wooded, swampy lands.

> Southeastern Minnesota, southern Michigan, western New York (local), and southern New Jersey (rarely) south to central Florida and Gulf Coast.

Prothonotary Warbler

27. SEE VI B b(2) 1 and IX A a(5) 2

House Sparrow

28. SEE IV A a(2) 2   **Purple Grackle**

B. Nesting in Colonies, Usually in Martin-houses

1. Nest of leaves, twigs, straw, feathers, bits of string, rags, and paper, sometimes with a little mud as foundation.

> Gulf of Mexico north throughout eastern and central United States.

Purple Martin

IX. In or On Buildings

A. Outside

a(1). On flat roofs
    1. SEE Nests On or In the Ground I A a(6) 1 and
      IV B 8   **Nighthawk**

a(2). On shelf or projection
    1. SEE VIII A a(3) 21 and Nests On or In the
      Ground II A a(1) 5 and II B b(1) 2
                         Carolina Wren

    2. SEE IV A a(1) 1 and IV B b(3) 1   **Robin**

    3. SEE VIII A a(2) 2   **Barn Owl**

a(3). Beneath eaves
    1. SEE IV B b(1) 2   **(Northern) Cliff Swallow**

    2. SEE VIII A a(3) 18 and IX A a(5) 4
                         House Wren

a(4). On wall
    1. SEE IV B b(2) 1   **Eastern Phoebe**

a(5). In a corner or cornice
    1. SEE V B b(2) 2   **Arkansas Kingbird**

    2. SEE VI B b(2) 1 and VIII A a(3) 27
                        House Sparrow

3. SEE VIII A a(1) 1   **Flicker**

4. SEE VIII A a(3) 18 and IX A a(3) 2
       House Wren

a(6). On chimney
1. SEE VII A 5   **Osprey**

B. Inside

b(1). On a rafter
1. SEE IV B b(1) 1   **Barn Swallow**

b(2). In a chimney
1. SEE VII C c(2) 1   **Chimney Swift**

(For Index of Birds see page 15)

1. The nest of the **Bobolink,** built among the tall grass of meadows, is very difficult to find (page 32).

2. The nest of the **Vesper Sparrow** is a thick rimmed, well cupped but not tightly woven structure (page 32).

Ruth Turner

3. While the **Field Sparrow** may build its nest of grasses on the ground, it frequently selects a site just above the ground in a low bush or brier patch (page 33).

4. The nest of the **Ring-necked Pheasant** is a slight natural hollow in grass or grainfield and lined scantily with leaves, grass and straw (page 34).

Hal H. Harrison

Wm. H. Lawrence

5. The **Killdeer** seems generally to prefer to rear its young about cultivated land and gardens where insects are abundant (page 35).

6.

The nest of the **Spotted Sandpiper** is generally made in the shelter of high weeds or grass (page 35).

Hal H. Harrison

Alfred O. Gross

7. A shallow depression in the forest floor lined with dead leaves serves as a nest for the **Ruffed Grouse** (page 38).

Hal H. Harrison

8.
The nest of the **Louisiana Water Thrush** is carefully hidden in a cavity in a brook bank (page 41).

S. A. Grimes

9. A **Carolina Wren** chooses a novel nesting site (page 39).

Hal H. Harrison

10.
The **Veery's** nest is
usually found on
the ground in low,
amp woods (page
9).

11.

The nest of the **Red-eyed Towhee** is exceedingly difficult to find because the materials used in its construction correspond both in color and texture with the immediate surroundings (page 43).

Hal H. Harrison

12.

The nest of the **Woodcock** is a mere depression in some dry spot in swampy ground (page 44).

Hal H. Harrison

13.

The **Whip-poor-will** lays its eggs among dead leaves, as if it were aware that they resemble so closely the color and pattern of the forest floor that only with difficulty can they be discovered (page 45).

Hal H. Harrison

Hal H. Harrison

14. Front view of **Ovenbird's** nest (page 47).

Hal H. Harrison

15.
The **American Bit-
ern** inhabits almost
impenetrable swampy
places where it builds
a practically flat plat-
form of dead flags
(page 49).

16.
The tops of growing flags are often interlaced over the nest of the **Least Bittern** to shield the eggs from above (page 49).

Hal H. Harrison

17. The **Sora's** nest, well constructed of flags and grasses and perhaps only a few inches above the water, may be concealed by a canopy of flags and have a runway leading to it (page 50).

Lawrence H. Walkinshaw

18. The nest of the **Black Tern** is a careless structure of a few dead sedges and grass (page 52).

19.
The **Black Duck** regularly uses its own down and breast or flank feathers to line its nest (page 53).

S. A. Grimes

20. The nest of the **King Rail,** composed of grass and weeds, is placed on the ground in a marsh and is often fastened in a tussock of grass (page 54).

21.
Compact and slightly hollowed, the nest of the **Virginia Rail** is built in a tuft of reeds or grasses close to the water (page 54).

Hal H. Harrison

Hal H. Harrison

22. The **Willet** uses a mere depression in the ground in which to deposit its eggs (page 58).

23.
The **Swamp Sparrow** dwells in the deep recesses of marshy thickets (page 56).

Hal H. Harrison

24. The **Clapper Rail** carefully conceals its nest in high
grass of the salt marsh (page 60).

25. The **Black Rail** may nest in fields of rank grass and grain (page 61).

Roger T. Peterson

26. The nest of the **Laughing Gull,** though frequently
    a mere hollow in sand without concealment, is usu-
    ally rather well built and more or less hidden among
    thick, low vegetation (page 63).

27. Sometimes the **Common Tern** builds an elaborate
    nest but usually it makes only a mere depression in
    the beach sand (page 64).

Hal H. Harrison

Hal H. Harrison

28. The **Black Skimmer** lays its eggs without concealment on the open sands (page 65).

Hal H. Harrison

29.

e nest of the
ing Plover is
slight hollow
sand, some-
es lined with
bles, bits of
ll and drift-
od (page 66).

Alfred O. Gross

30. The nest of the **Double-crested Cormorant** is a loosely put together structure of sticks and weed stalks (page 69).

31. Compactly built and usually well cupped, the nest of the **Glossy Ibis** is quite unlike the clumsy platforms of the herons (page 72).

S. A. Grimes

32.

Globular nest of **Long-billed Marsh Wren** cut in half to show eggs and interior (page 72).

Hal H. Harrison

33.

The **Redwing** usually builds its nest in reeds and cattails but sometimes it will build in a grassy field (page 74).

Hal H. Harrison

34.

The nest of the **Redwing** is a bowl-shaped rather bulky affair, usually attached to reeds and cattails (page 74).

Hal H. Harrison

35.
The nest of the **Alder Flycatcher** is somewhat loosely finished, with a ragged appearance outside and below (page 74).

Hal H. Harrison

36.
The **Blue-headed Vireo** seeks the cool shade of pine or hemlock in which to build its nest (page 76).

Hal H. Harrison

37. The nest of the **Red-eyed Vireo** is a neat and handsome little basket and very durable (page 77).

38. **Red-eyed Vireo** nest with one speckled cowbird egg (page 77).

39. Thick-walled, of silver gray plant fibers, the nest of the **Yellow Warbler** is one to excite admiration (page 83 and fig. 47).

40. The nest of the **Wood Pewee** is a good example of a nest saddled on a branch (page 82).

41.
The nest of the **Redstart** is a beautiful, neat, cup-shaped structure (page 83).

Ralph E. Lawrence

42. The nest of the **Wood Thrush** is to be looked for in trees of damp woods and thickets (page 85).

Hal H. Harrison

43. Through a lack of orientation, a **Robin** became confused and constructed two nests until she finally settled on the one in which eggs were laid (page 85).

Hal H. Harrison

44. The nest of the **Bronzed Grackle** is similar to the robin's but larger (page 87).

45. Mud reinforced with grass and straw makes the nest of the **Barn Swallow** rival our structures of cement and steel (page 87).

Roger T. Peterson

46.
Usually the nest of the **Black-throated Green Warbler** is placed high in a conifer and well hidden among the needles (page 90).

Hal H. Harrison

47.
The nest of the **Yellow Warbler** is usually placed in shrubs or low in trees of lawns and orchards near water (page 83 and fig. 39).

Hal H. Harrison

Alfred O. Gr

48. The nest of the **Cedar Waxwing** is sometimes a very
    handsome structure (page 95).

49. In the absence of the female the male **Cardinal** feeds
    the young; otherwise she feeds them (page 96).

Ralph E. Lawrence

50. The nest of the **Olive-backed Thrush** is usually built in a spruce or fir tree (page 99).

51. The nest of the **Cooper's Hawk** is a clean, substantial structure of dried sticks and lined with chips of outer bark of pine or oak (page 105).

52. There is no better built or more substantial hawk's
nest than that of the **Red-shoulder** (page 105).

Hal H. Harrison

53. The **Crow** builds a large bulky nest of strong sticks and lines it with strips of grapevine bark, grasses, moss, and fine roots (page 107).

54. The **Black-crowned Night Heron** often selects a tall tree for a nesting site (page 109).

Allan D. Cruickshank

55. The nest of the **Blue Jay** is a bulky, carelessly built affair, with a ragged rim (page 111).

56.
The **Black-billed Cuckoo** builds its nest in a small tree or bush, usually within eight feet of the ground (page 115).

57.
The nest of the
**Eastern King-
bird,** though
somewhat rag-
ged and loose
exteriorly, is
nevertheless
well cupped and
brimmed (page
115).

Hal H. Harrison

58. The nest of the **Mockingbird** is a coarse, rather bulky
affair and is placed in a tangle of undergrowth, bush,
or low tree (page 116).

S. A. Grimes

Roland Campbell

59. Strips of grapevine bark used in the lining help to identify the bulky but well-built cradle of the **Catbird** (page 116).

60.
Orchards are favorite natural resorts of the **Bluebird** and furnish plenty of home-sites in the shape of hollow trunks or limbs of trees (page 125).

Hal H. Harrison

61. Hollowed gourds are favorite nesting sites of **Purple Martins** in the South (page 126).